138th Edition

Travel to Providence Rhode Island

2023
People Who Know
Publishing
Jack Ross

Copyright © 2023 People Who Know Publishing

All rights reserved. No part of this publication may be reproduced, distributed, or transmitted in any form or by any means, including photocopying, recording, or other electronic or mechanical methods, without the prior written permission of the publisher, except in the case of brief quotations embodied in critical reviews and certain other noncommercial uses permitted by copyright law.

Printed in the United States of America

This travel guide is for informational purposes only and does not constitute legal, financial, or professional advice. While every effort has been made to ensure the accuracy of the information provided, the author and publisher make no representations or warranties of any kind, express or implied, about the completeness, accuracy, reliability, suitability, or availability of the information contained in this book. The reader assumes full responsibility for any actions taken based on the information provided in this book.

People Who Know Publishing

Forward: In this book, People Who Know Publishing will provide a travel guide of 101+ things to see, do and visit in Providence Rhode Island. We strive to make our guides as comprehensive and complete as possible. We publish travel guides on cities and countries all over the world. Feel free to check out our complete list of travel guides here:

People Who Know Publishing partners with local experts to produce travel guides on various locations. We differentiate ourselves from other travel books by focusing on areas not typically covered by others. Our guides include a detailed history of the location and its population. In addition to covering all of the "must see" areas of a location such as museums and local sights, we also provide up-to-date restaurant suggestions and local food traditions.

To make a request for a travel guide on a particular area or to join our email list to stay updated on travel tips from local experts sign up here: https://mailchi.mp/c74b62620b1f/travel-books

Be sure to confirm restaurants, addresses, and phone numbers as those may have changed since the book was published.

About the Author:

Jack Ross is a college student who was born in Westchester County, NY. He's an expert on the local "in the know" tips of the area and is an authority on Westchester and its towns. He's been featured in several publications including Business Insider and CNBC for his books.

During his spare time, he writes, plays tennis and golf and enjoys all water sports (including his latest favorite, the eFoil). Jack also enjoys traveling and is a food connoisseur throughout Westchester. Jack travels consistently and has been to majority of the states in the U.S.

Sign up for our email list to get inside access to the towns and places we cover!
>> https://mailchi.mp/c74b62620b1f/travel-books
>> https://mailchi.mp/c74b62620b1f/travel-books

Table of Contents

Providence Rhode Island ....
Introduction i
History ii
Economy iv
Transportation Systems v
Neighborhoods vi
Food vii
Here are our ten favorite restaurant recommendations! viii
Nightlife x
Local Traditions & Customs xi
What to buy? xii
Finally, here are the five most famous people from the city! xiii
101+ things to do in the city xiv
1. Explore Waterplace Park. xvii
2. Attend a WaterFire event. xviii
3. Visit the Rhode Island School of Design (RISD) Museum. xviii
4. Take a stroll along Benefit Street. xx
5. Tour the Rhode Island State House. xxi
6. Wander around the historic College Hill neighborhood. xxii
7. Enjoy a meal on Federal Hill, Providence's Little Italy. xxiii
8. Visit the John Brown House Museum. xxiv
9. Take a bike ride along the East Bay Bike Path. xxv
10. Attend a performance at the Providence Performing Arts Center. xxvi
11. Visit the Roger Williams Park Zoo. xxvii
12. Explore the Providence Children's Museum. xxviii
13. Attend a festival on Federal Hill. xxx
14. Check out the Providence Athenaeum. xxxi
15. Take a gondola ride in Waterplace Park. xxxii
16. Visit the Culinary Arts Museum at Johnson & Wales University. xxxiii

17. Explore the RISD Nature Lab. xxxiv

18. Attend a concert at The Strand Ballroom & Theatre. xxxv

19. Discover local artists at AS220 galleries. xxxvi

20. Visit the Governor Henry Lippitt House Museum xxxvii

21. Explore the historic jewelry district. xxxviii

22. Attend a comedy show at Comedy Connection. xxxix

23. Take a scenic walk around India Point Park. xl

24. Explore the Museum of Natural History and Planetarium xli

25. Attend a Brown University sporting event. xliii

26. Visit the Providence Children's Film Festival xliv

27. Take a tour of the John Hay Library. xlvi

28. Explore the historic districts of Elmwood and South Elmwood xlvii

29. Attend a Providence Bruins hockey game. xlix

30. Take a walk through Roger Williams National Memorial l

31. Explore the Blackstone River Bikeway. lii

32. Attend a WaterFire Arts Center event. liii

33. Take a boat tour of Narragansett Bay. lv

34. Visit the Museum of Work and Culture in Woonsocket lvi

35. Explore the Providence Ghost Tour lviii

36. Attend a performance by the Rhode Island Philharmonic Orchestra lix

37. Take a cooking class at a local culinary school. lxi

38. Attend a film screening at the Providence French Film Festival lxii

39. Explore the Ladd Observatory. lxiv

40. Visit the Sprout CoWorking Art Gallery. lxv

41. Attend a poetry reading at a local cafe lxvii

42. Take a tour of the historic Fox Point neighborhood. lxviii

43. Explore the Providence Art Club. lxx

44. Attend a WaterFire Full Lighting ceremony lxxi

45. Take a Providence Riverboat Company cruise lxxiii

46. Attend a play at the Wilbury Theatre Group lxxiv

47. Explore the Wanskuck Historic District. lxxvi
48. Attend the Rhode Island International Film Festival. lxxvii
49. Take a day trip to Newport. lxxix
50. Explore the Jewelry District Riverwalk. lxxxi
51. Attend a WaterFire Basin Lighting event. lxxxiii
52. Explore the Hope Street Farmers Market..lxxxv
53. Attend a drag show at The Dark Lady. lxxxvii
54. Visit the John Brown Memorial Park. lxxxviii
55. Explore the East Side Marketplace. lxxxix
56. Visit the Providence Magic Museum. xc
57. Attend a concert at Lupo's Heartbreak Hotel. xci
58. Take a scenic drive along Ocean Drive...xcii
59. Attend a performance at the Trinity Repertory Company. xciii
60. Explore the Roger Williams Botanical Center. xciv
61. Attend a WaterFire WaterFire for Recovery event. xcv
62. Take a hike in Lincoln Woods State Park. xcvi
63. Visit the Roger Williams Park Carousel Village. xcvii
64. Explore the Thayer Street shopping district..xcviii
65. Attend a WaterFire Clear Currents event. c
66. Visit the Governor Sprague Mansion Museum. ci
67. Explore the Ten Mile River Greenway. cii
68. Attend a show at the Providence Improv Guild. ciii
69. Take a walk through Swan Point Cemetery. civ
70. Explore the West Side Marketplace. cv
71. Attend a Providence Roller Derby match..cvi
72. Attend the Federal Hill Summer Festival..cvii
73. Take a historical walking tour of Providence. cviii
74. Attend a WaterFire Salute to Veterans event. cix
75. Explore the Providence Arcade, the oldest shopping mall in the U.S..........cx
76. Take a day trip to Block Island. cxi

77. Attend a WaterFire FireBall event. cxii
78. Explore the Roger Williams National Memorial Visitor Center. cxiii
79. Take a Providence Segway Tour. cxiv
80. Attend a WaterFire Basin Lighting: New Year's Eve event. cxv
81. Explore the Kennedy Plaza skating rink in winter. cxvi
82. Attend a Providence College basketball game. cxvii
83. Take a walk through the historic Smith Hill neighborhood. cxviii
84. Visit the RISD Fleet Library. cxix
85. Attend a concert at the Dunkin' Donuts Center. cxx
86. Explore the Blackstone River Valley National Historical Park. cxxi
87. Attend a WaterFire ArtMart event. cxxii
88. Take a cruise with Save The Bay. cxxiii
89. Attend a performance at the Firehouse Theater. cxxiv
90. Explore the Scituate Reservoir area. cxxv
91. Attend the Providence Anarchist Book Fair. cxxvi
92. Take a Providence Pedestrian Bridge walk. cxxvii
93. Explore the Pawtucket Arts Collaborative. cxxix
94. Attend a show at the Columbus Theatre. cxxx
95. Take a Providence Neighborhood Plant Walk. cxxxii
96. Visit the Pawtucket Wintertime Farmers Market. cxxxiii
97. Explore the Washington Secondary Bike Path. cxxxv
98. Attend a performance at the Providence Ballet Theatre. cxxxvi
99. Take a food tour of Federal Hill. cxxxviii
100. Explore the Neutaconkanut Hill Conservancy. cxxxix
101. Attend a Providence Gay Men's Chorus concert. cxli
102. Take a scenic drive through Foster, Rhode Island. cxlii
103. Attend a WaterFire Clear Currents: A Symposium on WaterFire event..cxliv
104. Explore the North Burial Ground. cxlvi
105. Visit the Slater Mill Historic Site. cxlvii
106. Attend the Gaspee Days Parade. cxlix

107. Take a stroll through DePasquale Square. cli
108. Explore the Slater Park Zoo in Pawtucket. cliii
109. Attend a WaterFire Tribute to the Olympics event. cliv
110. Take a day trip to Providence Plantations. clvi
Conclusion clix
References clxi

Travel to Providence Rhode Island

Providence Rhode Island

State: Rhode Island
Population: 190,934
Ranking in U.S.: N/A
County: Providence County
Founded: 1832
Tag line: N/A

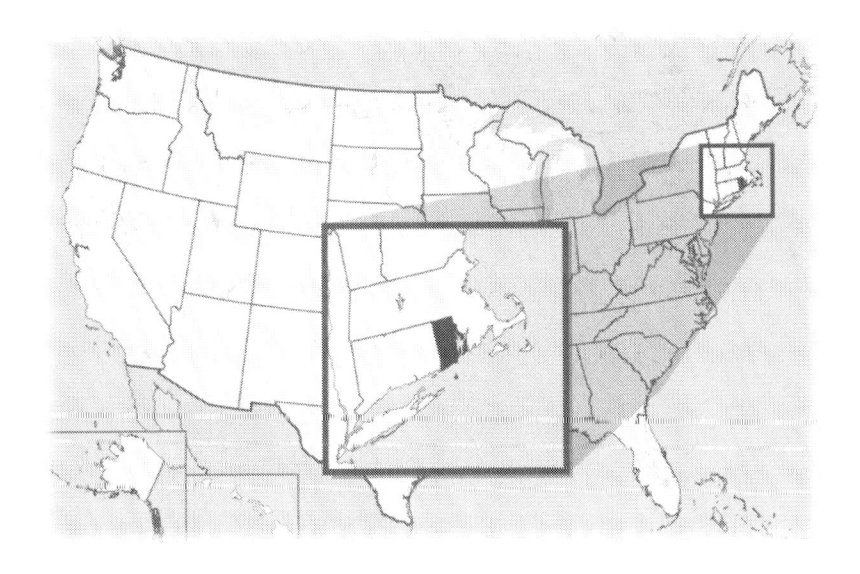

Introduction

"Providence combines the charm of a small town with the culture of a big city." - Unknown

Providence, the capital city of the smallest state in the United States, Rhode Island. Nestled along the scenic Narragansett Bay, Providence boasts a rich history, vibrant culture, and a unique blend of old-world charm and modern innovation. As you explore its cobblestone streets, historic landmarks, and thriving arts scene, you'll discover a city that has seamlessly merged its colonial past with a dynamic present.

Founded in 1636 by Roger Williams, a dissenter from the Massachusetts Bay Colony, Providence has a legacy rooted in religious freedom and tolerance. Over the centuries, it has evolved into a diverse and welcoming community, earning its nickname as the "Creative Capital" for its flourishing arts and creative industries.

The city's architecture reflects its storied past, with colonial-era buildings standing alongside contemporary structures. Benefit Street, often referred to as the "Mile of History," is lined with well-preserved colonial homes, while WaterFire, a renowned public art installation, illuminates the downtown rivers with flickering bonfires, creating a magical atmosphere.

Providence is home to several prestigious institutions of higher learning, including Brown University and the Rhode Island School of Design (RISD), contributing to a youthful energy and intellectual vibrancy. The city's culinary scene is equally diverse, offering a mix of culinary delights, from upscale restaurants to food trucks serving delicious local fare.

Whether you're strolling through the scenic Waterplace Park, exploring the boutiques of Federal Hill, or attending a performance at the renowned Providence Performing Arts Center, the city invites you to experience its unique blend of history, creativity, and community. Providence is not just a destination; it's a living tapestry where the past and present converge to create an unforgettable experience.

Travel to Providence Rhode Island

History

Roger Williams, a Puritan minister who was banished from the Massachusetts Bay Colony due to his religious beliefs, founded Providence in 1636. He sought a haven for religious freedom and tolerance and purchased land from the Narragansett tribe. Williams advocated for the separation of church and state, and his principles laid the groundwork for the concept of religious freedom and the First Amendment.

Providence's economy flourished in the 18th century, driven by maritime trade, shipping, and manufacturing. The city became a major hub for the transatlantic slave trade, and the Brown family, among others, gained significant wealth from this trade.

Before European settlers arrived, the area that is now Providence was inhabited by the Narragansett and Wampanoag Native American tribes. Roger Williams, the founder of Providence, established early contact and learned the native languages, fostering a degree of peaceful coexistence.

Travel to Providence Rhode Island

The late 19th and early 20th centuries saw an influx of immigrants, particularly from Ireland and Italy, contributing to the cultural diversity of Providence.
The city's neighborhoods, such as Federal Hill, became known for their distinct ethnic communities.

Travel to Providence Rhode Island

During the American Revolution, Providence played a role in supplying the Continental Army and became a center for manufacturing war materials. The Industrial Revolution brought further economic growth, with textile mills and factories transforming the landscape.

Like many American cities, Providence faced urban challenges in the mid-20th century, leading to urban renewal efforts. Some historic buildings were lost during this period. The 1970s marked a renaissance with the creation of WaterFire, an art installation that brought renewed attention to the city's waterfront.

Today, Providence is known for its institutions of higher learning, including Brown University and the Rhode Island School of Design (RISD), contributing to a vibrant intellectual and artistic community.
The city has continued to evolve, balancing preservation of its historic character with contemporary development initiatives.

Economy

Education and Healthcare:
The presence of renowned institutions like Brown University and the Rhode Island School of Design (RISD) contributes significantly to the local economy. Healthcare institutions, including major hospitals and research centers, also play a crucial role.

Creative and Design Industries:
Providence is often referred to as the "Creative Capital," and its economy benefits from a thriving arts and design community. RISD, in particular, has a significant impact on the creative sector.

Services and Financial Sector:
The services sector, including finance, insurance, and real estate, is an important contributor to the city's economy.
Providence has a diverse range of financial services and professional firms.

Tourism and Hospitality:
The city attracts tourists with its historical sites, cultural events, and waterfront areas.
WaterFire, a popular art installation, is a major draw for visitors.

Manufacturing and Industry:
While manufacturing has declined from its historical prominence, there are still some manufacturing activities in the region, albeit on a smaller scale.

Technology and Innovation:
Providence has seen efforts to foster a more innovative economy, with a growing focus on technology and entrepreneurship.
The presence of universities contributes to research and development initiatives.

Real Estate and Development:
Urban development projects have aimed to revitalize certain neighborhoods, balancing the preservation of historic structures with modern development.

Travel to Providence Rhode Island

Transportation Systems

Public Transit:
RIPTA (Rhode Island Public Transit Authority): RIPTA provides bus services throughout the state, including extensive coverage in Providence. The bus system connects various neighborhoods within the city and extends to neighboring towns and cities.

Rail Services:
Amtrak: Providence is served by Amtrak's Northeast Corridor, offering rail services to major cities such as Boston and New York City.
MBTA Commuter Rail: The Massachusetts Bay Transportation Authority (MBTA) commuter rail system connects Providence with cities in Massachusetts.

Roads and Highways:
Providence is well-connected by roadways, including Interstate 95, which passes through the city. This major highway facilitates travel between cities along the East Coast.
Local roads and bridges provide access to different neighborhoods within the city.

Biking and Walking:
Providence has made efforts to become more pedestrian and bike-friendly. There are bike lanes and paths throughout the city, and initiatives promote walking and cycling as sustainable modes of transportation.

T.F. Green Airport:
Located in Warwick, just south of Providence, T.F. Green Airport is a major regional airport serving domestic and international flights. It provides air travel options for residents and visitors.

Water Transportation:
While not the primary means of transportation, Providence's location on the Narragansett Bay has historically made water transportation important. Water taxis and ferries may operate in certain seasons, connecting different parts of the city and nearby islands.

Neighborhoods

Downtown:
The central business district with a mix of office buildings, shops, restaurants, and entertainment venues.
Home to landmarks such as the Rhode Island State House and Waterplace Park.

Federal Hill:
Known for its Italian-American community and a hub of great restaurants, cafes, and specialty shops.
The neighborhood hosts events like the annual Federal Hill Stroll.

East Side:
Home to Brown University and the Rhode Island School of Design (RISD).
Historic Benefit Street showcases well-preserved colonial architecture.
Thayer Street is a popular area for shopping, dining, and entertainment.

West End:
A diverse neighborhood with a mix of historic homes and a growing arts community.
Close to the Armory District, known for its historic armory building and artistic spaces.

Fox Point:
Located east of Downtown, known for its historic homes and proximity to the waterfront.
India Point Park offers scenic views of the harbor.

Travel to Providence Rhode Island

Food

Seafood:
As a coastal city, Providence is known for its fresh seafood. Local catches include clams, oysters, lobster, and fish. Popular dishes include clam chowder, stuffies (stuffed quahogs), and lobster rolls.

Italian Cuisine:
Federal Hill, known as the city's Little Italy, is a hub for Italian cuisine. You can find excellent pasta dishes, artisanal pizzas, and classic Italian desserts in this neighborhood.

Rhode Island-Style Pizza Strips:
A unique local pizza style, Rhode Island pizza strips are rectangular pieces of pizza dough topped with tomato sauce. They are often enjoyed at room temperature and are a popular party or snack food.

Hot Wieners:
A Rhode Island specialty, hot wieners are small, seasoned hot dogs served with a special meat sauce, chopped onions, mustard, and celery salt. They are often enjoyed "all the way."

Coffee Milk:
A popular local beverage, coffee milk is made by combining sweet coffee syrup with milk. It's a nostalgic and sweet drink that has its roots in Rhode Island.

Johnnycakes:
A traditional New England dish, Johnnycakes are cornmeal pancakes that have been enjoyed in the region for centuries. They are often served with butter and maple syrup.

Here are our ten favorite restaurant recommendations!

Al Forno:
Known for its innovative approach to Italian cuisine, Al Forno is famous for introducing grilled pizza to Providence. The restaurant emphasizes fresh, local ingredients.

Circe Restaurant & Bar:
Located in the heart of downtown Providence, Circe offers a stylish atmosphere and a diverse menu featuring contemporary American cuisine with Mediterranean influences.

Gracie's:
A fine dining establishment with a focus on locally sourced and seasonal ingredients. Gracie's offers an elegant setting and a tasting menu that highlights the culinary creativity of the chefs.

Los Andes:
A popular spot for Peruvian and Bolivian cuisine, Los Andes is known for its flavorful dishes, including ceviche, empanadas, and various grilled meats. The restaurant has a lively and vibrant atmosphere.

North:
An Italian-inspired restaurant with a focus on seasonal, locally sourced ingredients. North is known for its handmade pasta, wood-fired pizzas, and a diverse wine selection.

Nick's on Broadway:
A cozy and welcoming restaurant, Nick's on Broadway emphasizes farm-to-table dining. The menu features inventive dishes using fresh, local ingredients, and it's particularly known for its brunch offerings.

Travel to Providence Rhode Island

Persimmon:
An upscale restaurant offering modern American cuisine with a focus on locally grown and seasonal ingredients. Persimmon provides an intimate dining experience in a stylish setting.

Hemenway's Seafood Grill & Oyster Bar:
Renowned for its fresh seafood, Hemenway's offers a diverse menu featuring oysters, lobster, and other seafood delicacies. The restaurant has a classic New England seafood house ambiance.

Kabob and Curry:
Serving Indian and Pakistani cuisine, Kabob and Curry offers a flavorful and diverse menu. It is known for its delicious curry dishes, kebabs, and vegetarian options.

The Dorrance:
Housed in a historic building, The Dorrance is an elegant restaurant serving modern American cuisine. The menu features a mix of classic and contemporary dishes, and the ambiance is upscale and sophisticated.

Nightlife

The Hot Club:
A popular waterfront bar with a laid-back atmosphere. The Hot Club offers outdoor seating along the river, making it a great spot to enjoy drinks and beautiful views.

AS220:
An artist-run organization that includes a performance space, galleries, and a restaurant/bar. AS220 often hosts live music, art exhibitions, and other cultural events.

The Avery:
Located in the downtown area, The Avery is a stylish cocktail bar known for its craft cocktails and sophisticated ambiance.

Ego Providence:
A nightclub with multiple dance floors, Ego Providence is a go-to spot for those looking to enjoy a night of dancing to top DJs.

The Strand Ballroom & Theatre:
This historic venue hosts a variety of events, including live music concerts, dance parties, and other performances.

The Parlour:
A cozy bar with live music, The Parlour offers a relaxed setting and features local bands and musicians.

Travel to Providence Rhode Island

Local Traditions & Customs

WaterFire is a unique and iconic Providence tradition. This public art installation consists of a series of bonfires that are lit on the surface of the three rivers that pass through the downtown area. WaterFire events often include music and other performances, creating a magical and communal atmosphere.

Rhode Island Accent:
The local accent, sometimes referred to as the "Rhode Island accent," can be distinctive. Certain words and phrases may be pronounced in a way that reflects the region's linguistic nuances.

Historic Architecture:
Providence takes pride in its historic architecture, and residents often appreciate and preserve the unique character of older buildings. Historic neighborhoods, such as Benefit Street on the East Side, showcase well-preserved colonial-era homes.

College Culture:
With prestigious institutions like Brown University and the Rhode Island School of Design (RISD), Providence has a strong college culture. This influences the city's atmosphere, events, and intellectual pursuits.

Italian-American Heritage:
Federal Hill, known as Providence's Little Italy, celebrates Italian-American heritage. Residents often take part in events, festivals, and traditions that showcase the neighborhood's cultural richness.

What to buy?

WaterFire is a signature event in Providence, and you can find merchandise such as T-shirts, mugs, and prints featuring this iconic art installation.

Local Artwork and Crafts:
Visit galleries and craft markets to discover local artwork and handmade crafts created by Providence's talented artists. Look for paintings, sculptures, jewelry, and other unique pieces.

Rhode Island-themed Apparel:
Pick up clothing items like T-shirts, hats, or hoodies featuring Rhode Island or Providence-related designs. These items often showcase local pride and creativity.

Coffee Syrup:
Rhode Island has a unique tradition of enjoying coffee milk, made with sweet coffee syrup. Bring home a bottle of locally produced coffee syrup to recreate this Rhode Island favorite.

Quahog Jewelry:
Quahogs are hard-shell clams found in the region, and you can find jewelry made from quahog shells. Look for necklaces, bracelets, or earrings with these distinctive shells.

Local Foods:
Explore local markets for Rhode Island specialties like Del's Lemonade mix, Autocrat Coffee Syrup, and other regional treats. These make for delicious souvenirs or gifts.

Travel to Providence Rhode Island

Finally, here are the five most famous people from the city!

H.P. Lovecraft (1890-1937):
An influential writer in the horror genre, Howard Phillips Lovecraft was born in Providence. He is best known for his cosmic horror stories and the creation of the Cthulhu Mythos.

John F. Kennedy (1917-1963):
Although born in Brookline, Massachusetts, President John F. Kennedy spent a significant portion of his childhood in Providence. His family's home in the city is now a museum known as the John F. Kennedy National Historic Site.

Seth MacFarlane:
The creator of the animated television series "Family Guy" and "American Dad!" and the co-creator of "The Cleveland Show," Seth MacFarlane was born in Kent, Connecticut, but raised in Kent, Rhode Island, just outside of Providence.

Viola Davis:
Academy Award-winning actress Viola Davis was born in St. Matthews, South Carolina, but she attended Rhode Island College in Providence. Davis has received critical acclaim for her performances in films such as "The Help" and "Fences."

Eileen Farrell (1920-2002):
A renowned operatic soprano, Eileen Farrell was born in Willimantic, Connecticut, but she spent much of her childhood in Providence. She became a celebrated figure in the world of opera and classical music.

101+ things to do in the city

1. Explore Waterplace Park.
2. Attend a WaterFire event.
3. Visit the Rhode Island School of Design (RISD) Museum.
4. Take a stroll along Benefit Street.
5. Tour the Rhode Island State House.
6. Wander around the historic College Hill neighborhood.
7. Enjoy a meal on Federal Hill, Providence's Little Italy.
8. Visit the John Brown House Museum.
9. Take a bike ride along the East Bay Bike Path.
10. Attend a performance at the Providence Performing Arts Center.
11. Visit the Roger Williams Park Zoo.
12. Explore the Providence Children's Museum.
13. Attend a festival on Federal Hill.
14. Check out the Providence Athenaeum.
15. Take a gondola ride in Waterplace Park.
16. Visit the Culinary Arts Museum at Johnson & Wales University.
17. Explore the RISD Nature Lab.
18. Attend a concert at The Strand Ballroom & Theatre.
19. Discover local artists at AS220 galleries.
20. Visit the Governor Henry Lippitt House Museum.
21. Explore the historic jewelry district.
22. Attend a comedy show at Comedy Connection.
23. Take a scenic walk around India Point Park.
24. Explore the Museum of Natural History and Planetarium.
25. Attend a Brown University sporting event.
26. Visit the Providence Children's Film Festival.
27. Take a tour of the John Hay Library.
28. Explore the historic districts of Elmwood and South Elmwood.
29. Attend a Providence Bruins hockey game.
30. Take a walk through Roger Williams National Memorial.
31. Explore the Blackstone River Bikeway.
32. Attend a WaterFire Arts Center event.
33. Take a boat tour of Narragansett Bay.
34. Visit the Museum of Work and Culture in Woonsocket.
35. Explore the Providence Ghost Tour.
36. Attend a performance by the Rhode Island Philharmonic Orchestra.
37. Take a cooking class at a local culinary school.
38. Attend a film screening at the Providence French Film Festival.
39. Explore the Ladd Observatory.
40. Visit the Sprout CoWorking Art Gallery.

Travel to Providence Rhode Island

41. Attend a poetry reading at a local cafe.
42. Take a tour of the historic Fox Point neighborhood.
43. Explore the Providence Art Club.
44. Attend a WaterFire Full Lighting ceremony.
45. Take a Providence Riverboat Company cruise.
46. Attend a play at the Wilbury Theatre Group.
47. Explore the Wanskuck Historic District.
48. Attend the Rhode Island International Film Festival.
49. Take a day trip to Newport.
50. Explore the Jewelry District Riverwalk.
51. Attend a WaterFire Basin Lighting event.
52. Explore the Hope Street Farmers Market.
53. Attend a drag show at The Dark Lady.
54. Visit the John Brown Memorial Park.
55. Explore the East Side Marketplace.
56. Visit the Providence Magic Museum.
57. Attend a concert at Lupo's Heartbreak Hotel.
58. Take a scenic drive along Ocean Drive.
59. Attend a performance at the Trinity Repertory Company.
60. Explore the Roger Williams Botanical Center.
61. Attend a WaterFire WaterFire for Recovery event.
62. Take a hike in Lincoln Woods State Park.
63. Visit the Roger Williams Park Carousel Village.
64. Explore the Thayer Street shopping district.
65. Attend a WaterFire Clear Currents event.
66. Visit the Governor Sprague Mansion Museum.
67. Explore the Ten Mile River Greenway.
68. Attend a show at the Providence Improv Guild.
69. Take a walk through Swan Point Cemetery.
70. Explore the West Side Marketplace.
71. Attend a Providence Roller Derby match.
72. Attend the Federal Hill Summer Festival.
73. Take a historical walking tour of Providence.
74. Attend a WaterFire Salute to Veterans event.
75. Explore the Providence Arcade, the oldest shopping mall in the U.S.
76. Take a day trip to Block Island.
77. Attend a WaterFire FireBall event.
78. Explore the Roger Williams National Memorial Visitor Center.
79. Take a Providence Segway Tour.
80. Attend a WaterFire Basin Lighting: New Year's Eve event.
81. Explore the Kennedy Plaza skating rink in winter.
82. Attend a Providence College basketball game.

83. Take a walk through the historic Smith Hill neighborhood.
84. Visit the RISD Fleet Library.
85. Attend a concert at the Dunkin' Donuts Center.
86. Explore the Blackstone River Valley National Historical Park.
87. Attend a WaterFire ArtMart event.
88. Take a cruise with Save The Bay.
89. Attend a performance at the Firehouse Theater.
90. Explore the Scituate Reservoir area.
91. Attend the Providence Anarchist Book Fair.
92. Take a Providence Pedestrian Bridge walk.
93. Explore the Pawtucket Arts Collaborative.
94. Attend a show at the Columbus Theatre.
95. Take a Providence Neighborhood Plant Walk.
96. Visit the Pawtucket Wintertime Farmers Market.
97. Explore the Washington Secondary Bike Path.
98. Attend a performance at the Providence Ballet Theatre.
99. Take a food tour of Federal Hill.
100. Explore the Neutaconkanut Hill Conservancy.
101. Attend a Providence Gay Men's Chorus concert.
102. Take a scenic drive through Foster, Rhode Island.
103. Attend a WaterFire Clear Currents: A Symposium on WaterFire event.
104. Explore the North Burial Ground.
105. Visit the Slater Mill Historic Site.
106. Attend the Gaspee Days Parade.
107. Take a stroll through DePasquale Square.
108. Explore the Slater Park Zoo in Pawtucket.
109. Attend a WaterFire Tribute to the Olympics event.
110. Take a day trip to Providence Plantations.

Travel to Providence Rhode Island

1. Explore Waterplace Park.

Waterplace Park, nestled in the heart of Providence, is an expansive and beautifully designed urban oasis that offers a multifaceted experience for both residents and visitors. Positioned along the Woonasquatucket River, the park is best known for hosting the renowned WaterFire events that have become a signature of the city's cultural identity. The park's main attraction during WaterFire is the lighting of numerous bonfires that gracefully dance on the river, creating a mesmerizing and enchanting spectacle.

Apart from the captivating WaterFire events, Waterplace Park itself is a haven of tranquility with its cobblestone walkways, carefully landscaped green spaces, and picturesque pedestrian bridges. These elements collectively contribute to a serene and inviting atmosphere, providing an ideal setting for a leisurely stroll or a quiet moment of reflection.

The park's location is strategic, seamlessly blending with the surrounding urban environment while offering a retreat from the bustling city life. The cobblestone walkways wind through the park, providing a charming pathway along the riverbanks. As you explore, you'll encounter various public art installations that further enhance the park's aesthetic appeal and cultural significance.

The pedestrian bridges spanning the river not only serve as functional crossings but also present excellent vantage points to appreciate the scenic views of the water, the city skyline, and the architecture that surrounds the park. The juxtaposition of modern structures against the natural elements of the park creates a unique and harmonious landscape.

Waterplace Park is not just a destination for events or casual strolls; it serves as a dynamic space that hosts a range of activities throughout the year. From cultural festivals to art exhibitions, the park becomes a lively venue that fosters community engagement and a sense of togetherness.

Whether you're a resident looking for a peaceful escape or a visitor eager to immerse yourself in Providence's cultural tapestry, Waterplace Park stands as a testament to the city's commitment to creating spaces that are both aesthetically pleasing and socially vibrant. It's a place where nature, art, and community converge, offering an experience that is as diverse and rich as the city itself.

2. Attend a WaterFire event.

Attending a WaterFire event in Providence is an immersive and unforgettable experience that captures the essence of the city's artistic and cultural spirit. As the sun sets, the rivers running through Waterplace Park are transformed into a breathtaking display of light and fire. Numerous bonfires, set atop the water, cast a warm and ethereal glow, creating an enchanting ambiance that is both magical and communal.

The flickering flames are complemented by accompanying music and performances, enhancing the overall sensory experience. The carefully curated playlist adds a melodic backdrop to the visual spectacle, contributing to the unique and captivating atmosphere that defines a WaterFire event.

One of the remarkable aspects of attending a WaterFire event is the communal spirit it fosters. Locals and visitors alike gather along the riverbanks, bridges, and park pathways, sharing in the collective awe inspired by the dancing flames. The event serves as a cultural melting pot, bringing people together to appreciate art, music, and the beauty of the city's waterfront.

The scent of burning wood, the sound of crackling embers, and the reflection of firelight on the water create a multisensory experience that resonates with attendees long after the event concludes. Each WaterFire is distinct, often featuring themes or special dedications, making every visit a fresh and engaging encounter.

Whether you're strolling along the illuminated pathways, enjoying a boat ride on the river, or simply absorbing the vibrant energy of the crowd, attending a WaterFire event becomes a cherished memory that encapsulates the spirit of Providence's commitment to the arts and community. It's an occasion that transforms the cityscape into a living canvas, uniting diverse individuals under the enchanting glow of the flames, fostering a sense of connection and celebration.

3. Visit the Rhode Island School of Design (RISD) Museum.

A visit to the Rhode Island School of Design (RISD) Museum in Providence promises an enriching and culturally immersive experience. The museum,

Travel to Providence Rhode Island

affiliated with the renowned RISD, boasts a diverse and extensive collection of artworks spanning various periods, styles, and cultures. Nestled in the College Hill neighborhood, the museum itself is housed in an architecturally striking building that reflects the institution's commitment to creativity and artistic expression.

Upon entering the museum, you'll find yourself surrounded by a curated selection of paintings, sculptures, decorative arts, and textiles that showcase the breadth and depth of human creativity. The RISD Museum places a strong emphasis on educational engagement, and its exhibits often incorporate innovative displays and interpretive materials to enhance visitors' understanding of the artworks on display.

One of the distinctive features of the museum is its commitment to contemporary art, reflecting the forward-thinking ethos of RISD. Visitors have the opportunity to explore thought-provoking and cutting-edge exhibitions that highlight the intersection of tradition and innovation.

The museum's collection includes works from various cultures and time periods, providing a global perspective on art history. From ancient artifacts to modern masterpieces, each piece contributes to the rich tapestry of human creativity. Notable pieces by both established and emerging artists add to the museum's reputation as a dynamic hub for artistic exploration.

Beyond the galleries, the RISD Museum often hosts educational programs, workshops, and events that further connect visitors with the world of art. Whether you're an art enthusiast, a student, or someone simply curious about the creative realm, a visit to the RISD Museum is an opportunity to be inspired, challenged, and moved by the diverse expressions of human imagination.

As you explore the museum's halls, you'll encounter a thoughtfully curated journey through artistic movements, cultural expressions, and the evolution of creativity. It's a space where the boundaries of tradition and innovation blur, inviting visitors to engage with art in a way that transcends time and place. A visit to the RISD Museum is not just a stroll through galleries; it's an immersive exploration that leaves a lasting impression on those who seek to connect with the profound and transformative power of art.

4. Take a stroll along Benefit Street.

Taking a stroll along Benefit Street in Providence is like stepping into a living history book. This historic thoroughfare, often referred to as the "Mile of History," is renowned for its well-preserved architecture and charming cobblestone sidewalks. As you amble down Benefit Street, you'll find yourself surrounded by a captivating ensemble of Colonial, Federal, and Victorian-style houses, each with its own unique character and story to tell.

The street is lined with towering elm trees, casting a dappled shade that adds to the picturesque ambiance. Notable landmarks punctuate the landscape, including the John Brown House, a majestic mansion that stands as a testament to the city's colonial past. The street's rich history is further accentuated by the presence of historic churches, such as the First Unitarian Church with its distinctive steeple.

One of the fascinating aspects of Benefit Street is its collection of "milestones" or historic markers that provide insights into the significance of various buildings and their former residents. These markers serve as informative signposts, allowing you to trace the footsteps of Providence's early inhabitants and the prominent figures who shaped the city's identity.

The street's proximity to Brown University adds to its academic and intellectual ambiance. The architecture seamlessly blends with the vibrant energy of the university community, creating a dynamic and culturally rich environment.

The stroll along Benefit Street is not just a visual feast; it's a sensory experience that transports you to different eras. The cobblestone sidewalks echo with the footsteps of generations past, and the well-maintained facades evoke a sense of timelessness. During certain seasons, the street comes alive with the colors of blooming flowers and the rustling of leaves, enhancing the overall charm of the walk.

As you explore Benefit Street, you may find yourself drawn to the wrought-iron fences, hidden gardens, and other architectural details that add to the street's allure. It's a journey through both the architectural evolution of Providence and the narratives of the people who have called this historic street home.

In essence, taking a stroll along Benefit Street is an opportunity to connect with the soul of Providence, appreciating the city's deep-rooted history and the enduring beauty of its architectural treasures. Whether you're a history enthusiast, an architecture buff, or simply someone seeking a peaceful and

Travel to Providence Rhode Island

visually captivating experience, Benefit Street offers a delightful and enriching stroll through the heart of Providence's historic landscape.

5. Tour the Rhode Island State House.

Touring the Rhode Island State House in Providence is a journey into the heart of the state's government and a chance to appreciate the architectural and historical significance of this iconic building. Perched atop Smith Hill, the State House commands attention with its neoclassical design, a blend of Beaux-Arts and Greek Revival styles. The majestic white dome, topped with a bronze statue of the Independent Man, is a prominent symbol of Rhode Island's commitment to freedom and independence.

Upon entering the State House, visitors are greeted by a grand marble rotunda adorned with impressive murals that depict significant events in the state's history. The building's interior reflects a sense of elegance and civic pride, with polished marble floors, intricate woodwork, and ornate chandeliers contributing to its stately atmosphere.

Guided tours of the State House offer a comprehensive exploration of its various chambers and halls. The House of Representatives and Senate chambers showcase beautiful murals, while the State Library and offices display historical artifacts and documents. Visitors often have the opportunity to stand on the marble steps of the Grand Staircase, a location that has been witness to many significant events and speeches throughout Rhode Island's history.

One of the highlights of the tour is the State Room, a ceremonial space adorned with portraits of past governors and significant works of art. The Governor's Reception Room is equally impressive, featuring elaborate furnishings and historic artifacts that provide insight into the state's political legacy.

Beyond the architectural and artistic marvels, the Rhode Island State House stands as a living testament to the state's commitment to open government. The rotunda's "Liberty Arming the Patriot" statue and the "Independence" mural are poignant reminders of Rhode Island's role in the fight for liberty.

Touring the Rhode Island State House is not merely an exploration of a government building; it's an immersive journey into the state's history, values, and civic identity. It offers a glimpse into the workings of the government, the individuals who have shaped its trajectory, and the enduring principles of freedom that the State House represents. Whether you're interested in history, architecture, or civic affairs, a visit to the Rhode Island State House provides a captivating and educational experience that resonates with the spirit of the state.

6. Wander around the historic College Hill neighborhood.

Wandering around the historic College Hill neighborhood in Providence is a delightful journey through time and architecture. As you explore the narrow, tree-lined streets and brick sidewalks, you'll be transported to a bygone era characterized by well-preserved Colonial, Federal, and Victorian homes. The neighborhood is home to some of the city's oldest structures, creating an atmosphere that exudes charm and historical significance.

College Hill is anchored by Brown University, which contributes to the vibrant and academic ambiance of the area. The campus itself is adorned with historic buildings and open green spaces, inviting exploration and contemplation. The architecture of Brown University seamlessly integrates with the surrounding residential structures, creating a cohesive and visually appealing landscape.

Thayer Street, the main thoroughfare, buzzes with activity and is a hub for shopping, dining, and cultural experiences. Quaint bookstores, coffee shops, and boutiques line the street, providing a perfect blend of modern amenities and historic charm. The lively atmosphere is heightened by the presence of students, residents, and visitors, creating a dynamic and energetic vibe.

Benefit Street, a prominent avenue within the College Hill neighborhood, is particularly noteworthy. It features a remarkable collection of 18th- and 19th-century homes, including the impressive John Brown House, which stands as a testament to Providence's colonial history. The streetscape is enriched by the presence of antique street lamps, wrought-iron fences, and meticulously maintained gardens.

The hidden gems and architectural details that reveal themselves as you wander through College Hill contribute to the neighborhood's allure. From hidden gardens and ivy-covered walls to historic markers that provide insights into the area's past, each step unravels a new facet of Providence's rich history.

As you ascend the hill, panoramic views of the city unfold, offering a picturesque backdrop that enhances the overall experience. The neighborhood's elevated position provides an opportunity to appreciate the cityscape and the convergence of historic and contemporary elements that define Providence.

Wandering through College Hill is not just a visual feast; it's an immersive journey that allows you to connect with the city's cultural roots. Whether you're captivated by architecture, interested in history, or simply seeking a peaceful stroll, College Hill offers a quintessential Providence experience that captures the essence of this historic and intellectually vibrant neighborhood.

7.Enjoy a meal on Federal Hill, Providence's Little Italy.

Indulging in a meal on Federal Hill, Providence's Little Italy, is a culinary adventure that promises a rich tapestry of flavors and a warm, inviting atmosphere. As you step into this historic neighborhood, you're greeted by a vibrant scene of Italian restaurants, cafes, and delis that collectively create an immersive experience reminiscent of Italy's culinary traditions.

The aroma of garlic, herbs, and simmering sauces wafts through the air as you explore the diverse dining options. Federal Hill is renowned for its authentic Italian cuisine, and you'll find establishments ranging from cozy family-owned trattorias to upscale restaurants offering a contemporary twist on classic dishes.

Pasta lovers will be in their element with an array of choices, from handmade ravioli to perfectly al dente spaghetti. Traditional dishes like Osso Buco, Eggplant Parmesan, and Chicken Marsala showcase the depth and authenticity of Italian flavors. Many restaurants take pride in using fresh, locally sourced ingredients to enhance the quality and authenticity of their offerings.

Beyond pasta and main courses, be sure to explore the delectable world of Italian desserts. Tiramisu, cannoli, and panna cotta are just a few of the tempting treats that await those with a sweet tooth. Pair your meal with a fine Italian wine or indulge in a classic espresso to complete the dining experience.

The ambiance on Federal Hill is equally enticing. Whether you choose an intimate eatery with dim lighting and cozy booths or a bustling trattoria with lively conversations, each restaurant contributes to the neighborhood's warm and convivial atmosphere. In the evenings, the streets are often adorned with twinkling lights, creating a charming setting for a romantic dinner or a lively gathering with friends.

The restaurant owners and staff on Federal Hill take pride in preserving and sharing their Italian heritage through the culinary arts. Many establishments have been passed down through generations, adding a sense of familial tradition to the dining experience.

In essence, enjoying a meal on Federal Hill is not just about savoring exceptional Italian cuisine; it's a cultural immersion that allows you to partake in the rich tapestry of traditions, flavors, and hospitality that define Providence's Little Italy. Whether you're a connoisseur of Italian cuisine or simply seeking a memorable dining experience, Federal Hill beckons with open arms and a table set for an authentic taste of Italy in the heart of Rhode Island.

8. Visit the John Brown House Museum.

Visiting the John Brown House Museum in Providence is a step back in time to explore the rich history and architectural splendor of one of Rhode Island's most significant landmarks. The John Brown House, an imposing mansion built in the mid-18th century, stands as a testament to the wealth and influence of the Brown family, prominent figures in the state's history.

As you enter the museum, you're greeted by knowledgeable guides who provide insights into the house's storied past. The interior, adorned with period-appropriate furnishings and decor, offers a glimpse into the lifestyle of a prosperous colonial family. The John Brown House is renowned for its Georgian architecture, and each room reflects the elegance and sophistication of the era.

The museum provides a curated narrative of the Brown family's involvement in various aspects of Rhode Island's history, including trade, politics, and the abolitionist movement. The family's legacy is intricately woven into the fabric of the state, and the museum serves as a captivating repository of stories and artifacts that bring their history to life.

The guided tour takes you through the various rooms, including the opulent ballroom, family parlors, and bedrooms adorned with period-appropriate furnishings. Notable artifacts, portraits, and historical documents offer a nuanced understanding of the Brown family's contributions to the economic and social development of Rhode Island.

Beyond the architectural and historical aspects, the John Brown House Museum often hosts special events, lectures, and exhibitions that further enrich the visitor experience. The museum's commitment to education and preservation is evident in its efforts to showcase both the grandeur and complexities of colonial life.

Surrounded by well-maintained gardens and situated in the historic College Hill neighborhood, the John Brown House is not only a museum but also an integral part of Providence's cultural landscape. The picturesque exterior, characterized by its distinctive gambrel roof and Palladian windows, adds to the overall charm of the visit.

Whether you're a history enthusiast, an architecture buff, or someone intrigued by the stories of influential families, a visit to the John Brown House Museum provides an immersive and educational experience. It's an opportunity to connect with the past, appreciate the cultural heritage of Rhode Island, and gain insights into the lives of those who played a pivotal role in shaping the state's history.

9.Take a bike ride along the East Bay Bike Path.

Embarking on a bike ride along the East Bay Bike Path in Providence offers a scenic and refreshing outdoor experience, allowing you to soak in the natural beauty and recreational offerings along the route. Stretching approximately 14.5 miles from Providence to Bristol, this picturesque trail follows the shores of Narragansett Bay, providing breathtaking views of the water and surrounding landscapes.

Starting your journey in Providence, the path takes you through India Point Park, offering a delightful blend of urban and natural scenery. The trail is well-maintained, with smooth pavement making for a comfortable ride. As you pedal along, you'll encounter lush greenery, charming coastal vistas, and the soothing sounds of the bay.

Heading south, you'll pass through the Riverside and Crescent Park neighborhoods, where the path meanders along the shoreline. The sights include sailboats bobbing in the water, parks for picnicking, and opportunities to pause and appreciate the serenity of the bay.

The East Bay Bike Path is a haven for nature enthusiasts, providing glimpses of wildlife and birdwatching opportunities. The route also passes through Colt State Park, a scenic expanse with manicured lawns and walking trails, offering a perfect spot to take a break and enjoy a picnic.

As you continue toward Bristol, the trail leads you through charming coastal communities, each with its own character and landmarks. The final stretch brings you to Colt State Park and eventually to Independence Park in Bristol, where you can savor the waterfront atmosphere and perhaps explore the town's historic streets.

Whether you're an avid cyclist seeking a challenging ride or someone looking for a leisurely outdoor activity, the East Bay Bike Path accommodates all skill levels. The ride not only provides physical exercise but also a peaceful escape from the bustle of city life, allowing you to immerse yourself in the natural beauty and coastal charm that define this part of Rhode Island.

Overall, a bike ride along the East Bay Bike Path is a perfect way to enjoy the outdoors, connect with nature, and appreciate the scenic wonders that make this route a favorite among cyclists and nature enthusiasts alike.

10. Attend a performance at the Providence Performing Arts Center.

Attending a performance at the Providence Performing Arts Center (PPAC) is an enchanting experience that combines the grandeur of a historic venue with the excitement of world-class entertainment. The PPAC, located in the heart of downtown Providence, stands as an architectural gem and a cultural hub that has been hosting a diverse range of performances for decades.

As you enter the opulent lobby, adorned with ornate chandeliers and classic decor, you're immediately immersed in the timeless elegance of the theater. The PPAC's historic charm, dating back to its opening in 1928, sets the stage for an evening of theatrical magic.

The venue hosts a variety of performances, including Broadway shows, concerts, ballets, and other live productions. Whether you're there to witness a Tony Award-winning musical, a captivating play, or a renowned artist's concert, the PPAC's stage comes alive with energy and creativity.

Travel to Providence Rhode Island

The acoustics and seating arrangements are designed to provide an immersive experience, ensuring that every seat in the house offers a clear view of the performance. The plush red velvet seats and the richly adorned interior create a sense of intimacy, drawing the audience into the unfolding spectacle on stage.

The PPAC's commitment to showcasing diverse and high-quality performances contributes to its reputation as one of the region's premier entertainment venues. The schedule often includes a mix of touring Broadway productions, local performances, and internationally acclaimed acts, catering to a broad spectrum of tastes and preferences.

Before the show, you may choose to explore the surrounding area, with its vibrant downtown atmosphere and nearby dining options. From the lobby's elegant ambiance to the anticipation as the lights dim and the curtain rises, attending a performance at the PPAC is an immersive cultural experience that transcends the ordinary.

Whether you're a seasoned theatergoer or a first-time attendee, the Providence Performing Arts Center offers a setting where artistry and entertainment converge, creating memories that linger long after the final curtain falls. It's an opportunity to be transported into the world of the performing arts, surrounded by the historic charm and modern allure that define this iconic venue in downtown Providence.

11. Visit the Roger Williams Park Zoo.

A visit to the Roger Williams Park Zoo in Providence promises a day filled with wildlife encounters, conservation education, and family-friendly fun. Situated within the expansive Roger Williams Park, the zoo has been a beloved destination since its establishment in 1872, making it one of the oldest zoos in the United States.

Upon entering the zoo, you'll find yourself immersed in beautifully landscaped exhibits that recreate natural habitats for a diverse array of animal species. From the enchanting faces of the giraffes in the Plains of Africa exhibit to the playful antics of the sea lions at Marco Polo's Adventure, each area offers a unique and engaging experience.

The Fabric of Africa exhibit showcases majestic creatures like elephants, zebras, and African lions, while the Faces of the Rainforest introduces visitors to a vibrant array of tropical birds, primates, and reptiles. The North America exhibit provides a glimpse into the ecosystems of the continent, featuring animals such as red pandas and harbor seals.

One of the highlights of the zoo is the award-winning Alex and Ani Farmyard, where visitors of all ages can interact with domestic animals like goats, pigs, and chickens. This hands-on experience adds an extra layer of enjoyment, especially for younger visitors.

The Roger Williams Park Zoo is not only a place for entertainment but also an educational resource. The zoo actively participates in conservation efforts and provides information about the importance of preserving biodiversity. Various educational programs, events, and behind-the-scenes tours enhance the learning experience for visitors.

Throughout the year, the zoo hosts special events, seasonal celebrations, and opportunities to engage with zookeepers. The Carousel Village, located adjacent to the zoo, offers additional family-friendly activities, including a vintage carousel and a train ride through the park.

As you explore the zoo, the lush landscaping and well-designed exhibits create a serene and immersive environment. The commitment to animal welfare and conservation is evident in the zoo's efforts to provide enriching habitats and contribute to global conservation initiatives.

A visit to the Roger Williams Park Zoo is not just an outing; it's a chance to connect with nature, learn about wildlife conservation, and enjoy the wonder of the animal kingdom. Whether you're a wildlife enthusiast, a family looking for a day of adventure, or someone seeking a peaceful stroll through beautifully curated exhibits, the zoo offers a memorable experience for visitors of all ages.

12. Explore the Providence Children's Museum.

Exploring the Providence Children's Museum is a delightful and interactive experience designed to spark the curiosity and creativity of young minds. Nestled in Providence's Jewelry District, this hands-on museum is dedicated to providing a dynamic and educational environment for children and their families.

Travel to Providence Rhode Island

Upon entering, you'll find a vibrant space filled with engaging exhibits and activities that cater to a range of ages and interests. The museum is thoughtfully designed to encourage exploration, problem-solving, and imaginative play.

One of the standout features is the Water Ways exhibit, where children can experiment with water flow, build dams, and explore the principles of fluid dynamics. The Water Ways area provides an exciting and sensory-rich environment that blends learning with play.

Another popular exhibit is the Climber, an indoor play structure that allows children to navigate through tunnels, climb walls, and discover hidden nooks. This area promotes physical activity, coordination, and social interaction, fostering both cognitive and motor skill development.

For the budding scientists, the Discovery Studio provides a space for hands-on experiments, exploration of scientific concepts, and creative problem-solving. Whether it's building structures, experimenting with magnets, or exploring light and shadow, this exhibit encourages a love for STEM (Science, Technology, Engineering, and Mathematics) subjects.

The museum's focus on art and creativity is evident in the "Our City" exhibit, where children can engage in collaborative projects, explore urban planning concepts, and express their artistic vision. This interactive cityscape allows young visitors to become architects, builders, and artists as they shape their own miniature community.

In addition to these exhibits, the Providence Children's Museum frequently hosts special events, workshops, and programs that cater to specific themes or educational goals. The museum's commitment to providing a dynamic and ever-evolving experience ensures that each visit offers something new and exciting.

The Providence Children's Museum is not just a play space; it's an educational resource that promotes learning through hands-on exploration. The thoughtful design, emphasis on creativity, and diverse range of exhibits make it a valuable destination for families seeking an engaging and enriching experience for their children. Whether it's a rainy day or an afternoon of family fun, the museum provides a stimulating environment where children can learn, create, and discover in a playful and supportive setting.

13. Attend a festival on Federal Hill.

Attending a festival on Federal Hill, Providence's Little Italy, is a vibrant and cultural celebration that immerses you in the lively atmosphere of this historic neighborhood. Federal Hill is known for its rich Italian heritage, and its festivals are a testament to the community's pride in preserving and sharing their traditions.

One of the most iconic festivals on Federal Hill is the Federal Hill Summer Festival, which typically takes place during the warmer months. The streets come alive with colorful decorations, lively music, and the delicious aroma of Italian cuisine wafting through the air. The festival showcases the best of the neighborhood's culinary offerings, with local restaurants setting up outdoor stalls to offer a tempting array of pasta dishes, pizzas, cannoli, and more.

Live entertainment is a focal point of the festivities, featuring traditional Italian music, dance performances, and sometimes even contemporary acts. The vibrant sounds and energetic performances create a joyful and celebratory ambiance, inviting attendees to join in the revelry.

Throughout the festival, the streets are adorned with booths selling Italian-themed merchandise, arts and crafts, and specialty products. Local artisans often showcase their talents, adding a touch of authenticity to the event. It's an excellent opportunity to explore the unique shops and boutiques that line the streets of Federal Hill.

The Federal Hill Summer Festival is just one example, and other events throughout the year, such as the Columbus Day Parade and the Federal Hill Stroll, provide additional opportunities to experience the neighborhood's festive spirit. These celebrations often attract both locals and visitors, fostering a sense of community and shared cultural heritage.

Whether you're savoring authentic Italian dishes, enjoying live performances, or simply strolling through the lively streets, attending a festival on Federal Hill is a dynamic and immersive experience. It's a chance to embrace the warmth of the community, partake in the joy of celebration, and appreciate the cultural vibrancy that defines this iconic neighborhood in Providence.

Travel to Providence Rhode Island

14. Check out the Providence Athenaeum.

Checking out the Providence Athenaeum is a journey into the heart of intellectual and literary heritage in Providence. Established in 1836, this historic library is located on Benefit Street, in the midst of the city's College Hill neighborhood. Stepping into the Athenaeum is like entering a sanctuary for literature and knowledge, where the ambiance reflects a rich history of intellectual pursuits.

The Athenaeum's architecture exudes a sense of timeless elegance. The exterior, with its Greek Revival facade and iconic columns, sets the stage for the treasures within. The interior maintains an atmosphere of scholarly refinement, with high ceilings, wooden bookshelves, and natural light filtering through large windows.

The library's collection spans a wide range of subjects, from classic literature to contemporary works, making it a haven for bibliophiles and researchers alike. The shelves are lined with carefully curated books, and the library's commitment to intellectual exploration is evident in its diverse and thoughtfully organized collection.

One of the notable features of the Athenaeum is its membership program, which allows individuals to access the library's resources and attend events. The reading rooms provide a quiet and contemplative space for study and reflection, fostering an environment conducive to intellectual pursuits.

The Athenaeum is not only a repository of books but also a cultural hub that hosts events, lectures, and exhibitions. The events often feature renowned authors, scholars, and artists, creating opportunities for the community to engage with intellectual discourse and artistic expression.

As you explore the library, you'll discover hidden corners, cozy reading nooks, and the famous silver-domed telescope used by Edgar Allan Poe. The sense of history is palpable, with the Athenaeum having served as a gathering place for literary luminaries and intellectuals throughout the years.

Beyond its literary significance, the Athenaeum's commitment to community engagement is evident in its outreach programs and educational initiatives. It strives to be a place where people of all ages and backgrounds can come together to celebrate the joy of reading, learning, and intellectual exploration.

Whether you're a book lover, a history enthusiast, or someone seeking a quiet retreat for intellectual pursuits, checking out the Providence Athenaeum is a rewarding experience. It's a testament to the enduring power of libraries as cultural institutions and guardians of knowledge, inviting you to step into a world where the written word takes center stage.

15. Take a gondola ride in Waterplace Park.

Taking a gondola ride in Waterplace Park is a romantic and picturesque experience that allows you to savor the beauty of Providence from a unique vantage point. Waterplace Park, with its cobblestone walkways and serene river setting, provides an idyllic backdrop for a leisurely gondola excursion.

As you embark on the gondola, you'll be gently rowed along the Woonasquatucket River and the Providence River by a skilled gondolier. The slow and graceful movement of the gondola allows you to appreciate the charming architecture of the city, the lush greenery along the riverbanks, and the art installations that dot the landscape.

The gondolier, often dressed in traditional attire, adds to the authenticity of the experience, regaling you with stories of the city's history and points of interest along the route. They may also serenade you with classic Italian songs, enhancing the romantic ambiance of the journey.

As you glide through Waterplace Park, you'll pass under iconic bridges and witness the enchanting sight of the bonfires being lit during WaterFire events, if your ride coincides with this spectacular display. The flickering flames reflecting on the water create a magical atmosphere that adds an extra layer of charm to the gondola experience.

Gondola rides in Waterplace Park are available for private bookings, making them an ideal choice for a romantic date, a special celebration, or a unique way to explore the city with loved ones. The intimate setting of the gondola, coupled with the scenic beauty of the park, makes for a memorable and relaxing experience that stands out as a highlight of your time in Providence. Whether you're seeking a romantic escapade or simply a tranquil excursion, a gondola ride in Waterplace Park offers a distinctive and enchanting perspective on the city's beauty.

Travel to Providence Rhode Island

16. Visit the Culinary Arts Museum at Johnson & Wales University.

Visiting the Culinary Arts Museum at Johnson & Wales University in Providence offers a fascinating journey through the history and evolution of culinary arts, showcasing the diverse and dynamic world of food and gastronomy. The museum, located on the university's Harborside Campus, provides a unique intersection of education, culture, and the culinary arts.

Upon entering the museum, you're welcomed into a world of culinary exploration. The exhibits span a wide range of topics, from the evolution of kitchen equipment and cooking techniques to the cultural significance of food. The museum's collection includes a diverse array of artifacts, memorabilia, and interactive displays that appeal to both food enthusiasts and those interested in the art and science of cooking.

One of the highlights is the extensive collection of culinary tools and equipment, which showcases the evolution of kitchen technology over the centuries. From antique cooking utensils to modern innovations, the exhibits offer a comprehensive look at how culinary tools have shaped the way we prepare and enjoy food.

The museum also delves into the cultural aspects of food, exploring the role of cuisine in various societies and highlighting the global influences that have shaped culinary traditions. Exhibits may feature artifacts related to specific cuisines, culinary trends, and the cultural significance of food in different regions.

For those interested in the history of hospitality and culinary education, the museum provides insights into the development of culinary schools and the professionalization of the culinary industry. Johnson & Wales University's own role in shaping culinary education is a prominent part of the museum's narrative.

Interactive displays and multimedia presentations add an engaging and educational dimension to the museum experience. Visitors have the opportunity to learn about the science behind cooking, explore virtual culinary journeys, and gain a deeper understanding of the artistry that goes into creating culinary masterpieces.

The Culinary Arts Museum at Johnson & Wales University serves as a valuable resource for students, professionals, and the general public, fostering an appreciation for the rich tapestry of culinary history and innovation. Whether you're a culinary enthusiast, a student of the culinary arts, or someone intrigued by the cultural significance of food, a visit to this museum offers a savory and enriching experience in the heart of Providence.

17. Explore the RISD Nature Lab.

Exploring the RISD Nature Lab is a unique and immersive experience that invites you to delve into the intersection of art, design, and the natural world. Located within the Rhode Island School of Design (RISD), the Nature Lab serves as a hub for creative exploration, offering students and visitors the opportunity to engage with the beauty and complexity of the natural environment.

The Nature Lab is not a traditional natural history museum; instead, it is a dynamic space that blurs the boundaries between science and art. As you enter, you'll encounter a diverse collection of specimens, ranging from taxidermy animals to botanical specimens, bones, shells, and other artifacts from the natural world. This eclectic array serves as a rich source of inspiration for artists, designers, and students seeking to understand and represent the intricacies of nature.

One of the distinguishing features of the Nature Lab is its emphasis on hands-on learning. Visitors are encouraged to handle and draw from the specimens, fostering a direct and tactile connection with the natural world. The lab provides drawing materials, microscopes, and other tools to facilitate observation and exploration.

The Nature Lab is not limited to static displays; it often hosts workshops, lectures, and events that bring in experts from various disciplines to share their insights. These sessions may cover topics such as scientific illustration, ecological awareness, or the intersection of biology and design, offering a dynamic and intellectually stimulating environment.

The space itself is designed to evoke a sense of wonder and curiosity. The atmosphere is conducive to both focused study and collaborative exploration, making it a valuable resource for RISD students and the broader community.

Whether you're an artist seeking inspiration from the natural world, a biology enthusiast eager to merge science with art, or simply someone curious about the intricate details of plants and animals, the RISD Nature Lab provides a captivating space for discovery. It's a testament to the power of interdisciplinary exploration and the idea that the natural world is a boundless source of inspiration for creative minds.

18. Attend a concert at The Strand Ballroom & Theatre.

Attending a concert at The Strand Ballroom & Theatre in Providence promises an electrifying and immersive live music experience. Situated in the heart of the city, The Strand is a historic venue with a rich legacy, and it has been a prominent space for entertainment and cultural events since its early days.

As you step into The Strand, you're greeted by a vibrant atmosphere, with the venue's historic architecture blending seamlessly with modern lighting and sound systems. The combination of the venue's historical charm and contemporary amenities creates an inviting space for music enthusiasts of all genres.

The Strand hosts a diverse lineup of concerts, featuring local and international artists across various musical genres. Whether you're into rock, pop, hip-hop, indie, or electronic music, The Strand offers a stage for a wide range of musical acts. The venue's schedule is often packed with performances by both emerging talents and established artists, ensuring there's always something for every music lover.

The acoustics and layout of The Strand are designed to provide an optimal viewing and listening experience. The venue boasts a spacious dance floor, tiered seating, and intimate VIP sections, allowing concertgoers to choose the vantage point that suits their preferences. The energy of the crowd, combined with the artist's performance, creates a dynamic and memorable atmosphere.

Beyond concerts, The Strand also hosts other events, including comedy shows, dance parties, and special events. The versatility of the venue makes it a cultural hub in Providence, catering to a broad spectrum of entertainment tastes.

Before or after the concert, the surrounding area offers a variety of dining options and nightlife, allowing you to make the most of your night out in downtown Providence. Whether you're a devoted fan following your favorite artist or someone looking for a lively night of music and entertainment, attending a concert at The Strand Ballroom & Theatre promises an unforgettable and immersive experience in the heart of the city's vibrant cultural scene.

19. Discover local artists at AS220 galleries.

Discovering local artists at AS220 galleries in Providence is a journey into the city's dynamic and diverse arts community. AS220 is a non-profit community arts organization that has been a driving force in supporting and showcasing emerging and established artists since its inception in 1985.

AS220's galleries serve as a platform for a wide range of artistic expressions, including visual arts, performance art, and interdisciplinary works. The organization is committed to providing accessible and inclusive spaces for artists to exhibit their creations and engage with the community.

The galleries feature rotating exhibitions that highlight the talents and perspectives of local artists. As you explore the exhibits, you'll encounter a rich tapestry of artistic styles, mediums, and themes, reflecting the vibrancy and diversity of the Providence arts scene.

The organization's commitment to fostering creativity extends beyond the gallery walls. AS220 offers studio spaces, live/work spaces, and resources for artists to develop and showcase their work. The collaboration between AS220 and the local artistic community has contributed significantly to Providence's reputation as a hub for creativity and innovation.

In addition to visual arts, AS220 hosts performances, live music, and events that further celebrate the artistic spirit of the community. The organization's dedication to inclusivity and accessibility makes it a welcoming space for artists and art enthusiasts alike.

Visiting AS220 galleries is not just an opportunity to view art; it's a chance to connect with the pulse of Providence's artistic scene. The eclectic mix of works and the emphasis on supporting local talent create an engaging and immersive experience for visitors. Whether you're a seasoned art aficionado or someone curious about the local creative scene, AS220 provides a dynamic and ever-changing space to discover and appreciate the talents of Providence's vibrant artists.

Travel to Providence Rhode Island

20. Visit the Governor Henry Lippitt House Museum.

Visiting the Governor Henry Lippitt House Museum in Providence offers a glimpse into the grandeur and history of the city during the Gilded Age. Located on the renowned College Hill, this meticulously preserved Victorian mansion provides a captivating window into the lifestyle of one of Rhode Island's prominent families.

Built in 1865, the Lippitt House is a stunning example of High Victorian architecture, designed by the renowned architect Thomas A. Tefft. As you approach the house, its distinctive features, including the ornate exterior detailing, towering windows, and expansive porch, evoke the opulence of the era.

The museum offers guided tours that take you through the various rooms, each meticulously restored to reflect the style and taste of the Lippitt family. The interiors showcase exquisite period furnishings, original artwork, and intricate architectural details that transport you back in time.

The Lippitt House served as the residence of Henry Lippitt, a successful industrialist, and politician who went on to become the Governor of Rhode Island. The house is not only a testament to Victorian design but also a reflection of the social and political history of the state during the late 19th century.

The guided tours provide insights into the family's history, the architectural significance of the house, and the cultural context of the Gilded Age. You'll explore various rooms, including the grand parlor, the elegant dining room, and the family bedrooms, each with its own story and connection to the Lippitt family's legacy.

Surrounded by well-manicured gardens, the Governor Henry Lippitt House Museum stands as a historical gem amidst the bustling College Hill neighborhood. The lush grounds and the imposing exterior contribute to the overall charm of the visit.

Whether you have an interest in history, architecture, or simply enjoy stepping into the past, a visit to the Governor Henry Lippitt House Museum provides a captivating and educational experience. It allows you to appreciate the craftsmanship of a bygone era and gain insights into the lives of the individuals who shaped Rhode Island's history during a pivotal period of economic and social transformation.

21. Explore the historic jewelry district.

Exploring the historic Jewelry District in Providence is a journey through the city's industrial past and a contemporary hub of innovation. Located just south of downtown, this district has been a crucial part of Providence's identity, particularly known for its historic significance in the jewelry and silverware industries.

Historical Context: The Jewelry District played a pivotal role in the city's economic development during the 19th and early 20th centuries. It was a thriving center for jewelry manufacturing, boasting numerous workshops and factories that contributed to Providence's reputation as the "Jewelry Capital of the World."

Architectural Heritage: As you wander through the district, you'll encounter a mix of historic buildings that once housed jewelry manufacturing facilities. The architecture reflects the industrial character of the area, with red-brick factories and warehouses showcasing the craftsmanship of a bygone era.

Knowledge District: In recent years, the Jewelry District has undergone transformation, evolving into the Knowledge District—a dynamic hub for education, research, and innovation. Brown University and the Rhode Island School of Design (RISD) have expanded their presence in this area, fostering a collaborative environment that bridges academia and industry.

Brown University's Alpert Medical School: One notable institution in the district is Brown University's Alpert Medical School. The modern design of the medical school building contrasts with the historic surroundings, symbolizing the district's evolution.

Innovation and Technology: The Jewelry District is also home to a burgeoning innovation and technology scene. The development of the Wexford Innovation Complex and the Cambridge Innovation Center has attracted startups, entrepreneurs, and research initiatives, creating a vibrant ecosystem focused on technology, life sciences, and healthcare.

Travel to Providence Rhode Island

Waterfront Parks: The district is situated along the Providence River, offering picturesque waterfront parks such as the Davol Square River Walk and the upcoming parks near the pedestrian bridge. These areas provide a tranquil escape and opportunities for outdoor activities.

Restaurants and Cafes: The Jewelry District features a variety of restaurants and cafes, making it a great place to enjoy a meal or a cup of coffee. The culinary scene reflects the district's transformation, with a mix of casual eateries and establishments catering to the academic and professional community.

Exploring the Jewelry District allows you to witness the convergence of history, innovation, and urban development. Whether you're interested in the city's industrial heritage, cutting-edge research, or simply enjoy a stroll along the waterfront, this district offers a multifaceted experience that captures the spirit of Providence's evolution.

22. Attend a comedy show at Comedy Connection.

Attending a comedy show at Comedy Connection in Providence guarantees an evening filled with laughter and entertainment. Located in the heart of the city, Comedy Connection has been a fixture in the local comedy scene for decades, providing a platform for both emerging and established comedians.

Intimate Setting: The venue's intimate setting creates a lively and engaging atmosphere, allowing the audience to feel close to the performers. The layout ensures that every seat in the house provides a good view of the stage, contributing to a shared experience of laughter and enjoyment.

Diverse Lineups: Comedy Connection hosts a diverse range of comedians, including both nationally touring headliners and up-and-coming talents. The variety in comedic styles and perspectives ensures that each show offers a fresh and entertaining experience.

Local Talent: Providence has a vibrant local comedy scene, and Comedy Connection often features performances by talented local comedians. This not only supports the community but also adds a unique flavor to the lineup.

Themed Nights and Special Events: The venue frequently organizes themed nights and special events, such as open mic nights, comedy competitions, and themed showcases. These events provide opportunities for new comedians to showcase their skills and for the audience to enjoy a diverse range of comedic performances.

Full-Service Bar: Comedy Connection typically offers a full-service bar with a selection of drinks, adding to the overall enjoyment of the evening. Many patrons appreciate the option to sip on a beverage while enjoying the comedy acts.

Proximity to Downtown: The central location of Comedy Connection makes it easily accessible from various parts of the city. Before or after the show, you can explore the vibrant downtown area, with its restaurants, bars, and nightlife options.

Date Night or Group Outings: Whether you're planning a date night, a fun outing with friends, or just seeking a good laugh, Comedy Connection provides an inclusive and entertaining environment suitable for various occasions.

Attending a comedy show at Comedy Connection is not just about the punchlines; it's an opportunity to unwind, share laughs with friends, and enjoy the comedic talents that grace the stage. With its rich comedic tradition and commitment to providing a welcoming space for laughter, Comedy Connection remains a beloved destination for comedy enthusiasts in Providence.

23. Take a scenic walk around India Point Park.

Embarking on a scenic walk around India Point Park in Providence promises a tranquil and picturesque experience along the waterfront. Located at the confluence of the Seekonk River and the Providence River, this park offers a serene escape within the city.

Waterfront Views: As you start your walk, you'll be greeted by stunning waterfront views. The park provides unobstructed vistas of the rivers, allowing you to watch boats sail by and enjoy the gentle ripples of the water.

Walking Trails: India Point Park features well-maintained walking trails that meander along the riverbanks. The pathways are surrounded by lush greenery and shaded areas, creating a pleasant environment for a leisurely stroll.

Travel to Providence Rhode Island

Bridges and Architecture: The park is situated near iconic bridges, including the Point Street Bridge and the Crawford Street Bridge. The architectural elements of these structures add character to the scenery and create photo-worthy moments.

Boat Launch and Marina: The park includes a boat launch and a marina, adding a dynamic element to the landscape. Watching boats come and go, or observing the serene marina, adds to the maritime charm of India Point Park.

Picnic Areas: Throughout the park, you'll find picnic areas with tables and benches. It's an ideal spot to bring a picnic and enjoy a meal with a view, whether you're solo, with a partner, or as part of a family outing.

Wildlife Spotting: The park's natural setting attracts various bird species and provides opportunities for wildlife spotting. Bring your binoculars, and you might catch glimpses of local birds and other river inhabitants.

Sunset Views: If you time your walk right, the park offers spectacular sunset views over the water. The changing colors of the sky and the reflection on the river create a serene and romantic ambiance.

Pedestrian Bridge: The park is connected to the East Bay Bike Path via the India Point Park Pedestrian Bridge. Crossing this bridge allows you to extend your walk and explore additional areas along the waterfront.

Community Events: India Point Park occasionally hosts community events, festivals, and outdoor concerts. Checking the local events calendar can add an extra layer of enjoyment to your visit.

Whether you're seeking a peaceful retreat, a scenic workout, or a romantic evening stroll, a walk around India Point Park provides a refreshing and rejuvenating experience along the waterfront, showcasing the natural beauty and charm that Providence has to offer.

24.Explore the Museum of Natural History and Planetarium.

Exploring the Museum of Natural History and Planetarium in Providence is a captivating journey through the wonders of the natural world and the vastness of the cosmos. Situated in Roger Williams Park, this museum offers a diverse range of exhibits and educational programs, making it a fascinating destination for visitors of all ages.

Natural History Exhibits: The museum's natural history exhibits feature a wide array of specimens, artifacts, and interactive displays that showcase the biodiversity of the Earth. From geological formations and fossils to exhibits on local ecosystems and wildlife, the museum provides a comprehensive look at the natural wonders of our planet.

Dioramas and Habitats: Immersive dioramas recreate various ecosystems, allowing visitors to step into scenes from the rainforest, the Arctic, and other habitats. These meticulously crafted displays provide insights into the interconnectedness of different species and their environments.

Dinosaur Exhibits: For those fascinated by prehistoric life, the museum's dinosaur exhibits offer a glimpse into the world of these ancient creatures. Life-sized models, fossils, and informative displays bring the age of dinosaurs to life.

Planetarium Shows: The museum's planetarium is a highlight, offering captivating shows that explore the night sky, celestial phenomena, and the wonders of our universe. Whether you're interested in astronomy or simply enjoy the beauty of the cosmos, the planetarium shows provide an immersive and educational experience.

Educational Programs: The museum hosts educational programs, workshops, and events for visitors of all ages. These programs cover a range of scientific topics, fostering a love for learning and discovery.

Meteorites and Minerals: The museum houses a collection of meteorites and minerals, allowing visitors to explore the geology of our planet and beyond. The exhibits provide insights into the formation of Earth and the cosmic origins of these intriguing specimens.

Interactive Learning: Many exhibits are designed with interactivity in mind, providing hands-on learning experiences for both children and adults. Whether it's touching fossils, manipulating interactive displays, or participating in workshops, visitors can engage with the material in a dynamic way.

Seasonal Events: The museum often hosts seasonal events, including special exhibits, workshops, and activities tied to holidays or natural phenomena. Checking the event calendar adds an extra dimension to your visit.

Beautiful Grounds: Located in Roger Williams Park, the museum is surrounded by beautiful grounds. After exploring the exhibits, visitors can enjoy a stroll in the park, visit the nearby zoo, or have a picnic in the serene outdoor spaces.

A visit to the Museum of Natural History and Planetarium offers a blend of education, exploration, and awe-inspiring moments that cater to a wide range of interests. Whether you're a science enthusiast, a family seeking an educational outing, or someone simply curious about the world around you, this museum provides a captivating experience in the heart of Providence.

25. Attend a Brown University sporting event.

Attending a Brown University sporting event in Providence provides an opportunity to witness high-caliber collegiate athletics in a vibrant and spirited atmosphere. Brown's athletic teams, known as the Bears, compete in the NCAA Division I Ivy League, and their home games showcase both competitive sportsmanship and enthusiastic school spirit.

Football at Brown Stadium: If you attend a Brown University football game at Brown Stadium, you'll experience the excitement of college football in a historic setting. The cheering crowd, marching band, and the energy of the players contribute to a thrilling game day experience.

Basketball at the Pizzitola Sports Center: The Pizzitola Sports Center hosts Brown University's basketball games. The venue provides an intimate setting, allowing fans to feel close to the action on the court. The enthusiastic atmosphere and passionate support from the crowd make basketball games particularly lively.

Hockey at Meehan Auditorium: For ice hockey enthusiasts, Meehan Auditorium is the place to be during Brown University hockey games. The fast-paced action on the ice and the camaraderie among fans create an electric atmosphere in this intimate arena.

Soccer and Lacrosse at Stevenson-Pincince Field: Stevenson-Pincince Field is the home venue for Brown's soccer and lacrosse teams. The open-air setting provides a picturesque backdrop for these outdoor sports, and the passionate fanbase adds to the spirited atmosphere.

Baseball at Murray Stadium: Brown's baseball team competes at Murray Stadium, offering a classic baseball experience. The stadium provides comfortable seating and an opportunity to enjoy America's pastime in a collegiate setting.

Softball at the Brown Softball Field: The Brown Softball Field hosts the university's softball games. The facility provides an intimate space for fans to support the team and enjoy the strategic and dynamic nature of the sport.

Track and Field at the Katherine Moran Coleman Aquatics Center: For track and field events, the Katherine Moran Coleman Aquatics Center often serves as a hub of athletic activity. The center's facilities support a range of events and competitions.

Spirit and Tradition: Attending a Brown University sporting event is not just about the games themselves; it's an opportunity to experience the school's spirit and traditions. From the Brown Band to the lively student section, each game is infused with the unique energy of the Brown community.

Community Engagement: Brown University sporting events often draw a diverse audience, bringing together students, alumni, faculty, and local residents. The sense of community and shared enthusiasm for the Bears create a welcoming and inclusive environment.

Whether you're a devoted sports fan, a proud alum, or someone looking for a lively and spirited experience, attending a Brown University sporting event is a fantastic way to immerse yourself in the excitement of collegiate athletics while enjoying the vibrant atmosphere of the Providence community.

26. Visit the Providence Children's Film Festival.

Visiting the Providence Children's Film Festival is a delightful and enriching experience that combines the magic of cinema with a focus on storytelling and

Travel to Providence Rhode Island

creativity for young audiences. This annual event, held in Providence, showcases a diverse selection of films specifically curated to engage and inspire children and families.

Diverse Film Selection: The festival features a carefully curated selection of films from around the world, spanning various genres and themes. From animated features to live-action films, the lineup caters to a wide range of interests and age groups.

Cinematic Exploration for Children: The Providence Children's Film Festival is designed to introduce children to the world of cinema in a thoughtful and age-appropriate manner. The films often explore themes of friendship, curiosity, diversity, and imagination.

Interactive Workshops: In addition to film screenings, the festival often hosts interactive workshops and activities. These may include hands-on filmmaking workshops, discussions with filmmakers, and opportunities for children to explore the creative aspects of storytelling and film production.

Cultural Exposure: The diverse selection of films provides children with exposure to different cultures, perspectives, and storytelling traditions. This can be an educational and eye-opening experience, fostering a sense of global awareness and empathy.

Family-Friendly Atmosphere: The festival creates a family-friendly atmosphere, encouraging parents and children to attend together. The shared experience of watching films and engaging in related activities strengthens family bonds and creates lasting memories.

Community Engagement: The Providence Children's Film Festival often involves the local community, including schools, libraries, and cultural organizations. This collaborative approach contributes to a sense of community engagement and shared appreciation for the arts.

Film Awards: Some festivals feature awards or recognitions for outstanding films, providing a platform to celebrate the achievements of filmmakers who create exceptional content for children.

Beautiful Venues: The festival venues, often located in the heart of Providence, add to the overall experience. The architecture and ambiance of these spaces enhance the magic of watching films on the big screen.

Yearly Tradition: Attending the Providence Children's Film Festival can become a yearly tradition for families, offering an anticipated and exciting event that adds to the cultural richness of the local community.

Whether you're a family with young children, an educator seeking educational and entertaining content, or simply someone with a passion for films that inspire and captivate young minds, the Providence Children's Film Festival provides a charming and engaging experience that celebrates the art of storytelling through cinema.

27. Take a tour of the John Hay Library.

Taking a tour of the John Hay Library in Providence is a journey into the world of rare books, manuscripts, and special collections. Part of Brown University, this historic library, located on Prospect Street, is an architectural gem that houses a treasure trove of literary and historical artifacts.

Architectural Beauty: The John Hay Library is an architectural marvel designed by the esteemed firm Shepley, Rutan, and Coolidge in the early 20th century. The building itself is a work of art, featuring elements of Renaissance and Gothic Revival styles.

Rare Book Collections: The library is renowned for its extensive collection of rare books and manuscripts. Visitors have the opportunity to explore centuries-old volumes, rare editions, and literary treasures that offer insights into the evolution of written knowledge.

Special Collections: The library is home to numerous special collections that encompass a wide range of subjects, including literature, history, art, and culture. These collections often include unique and valuable items that are not commonly found in standard libraries.

Manuscripts and Archives: For those interested in primary sources, the John Hay Library's manuscript and archival holdings provide access to letters, diaries, and other original documents that offer a firsthand glimpse into historical events and the lives of notable figures.

Haffenreffer Museum: The library houses the Haffenreffer Museum of Anthropology, which showcases artifacts from diverse cultures around the world. This museum within the library adds a multidisciplinary dimension to the overall experience.

Exhibition Spaces: The library often features rotating exhibitions that highlight specific themes, authors, or historical periods. These exhibitions provide curated insights into the depth and breadth of the library's collections.

Educational Programs: The John Hay Library occasionally hosts educational programs, lectures, and events that engage the community and promote a deeper understanding of the library's resources. These programs may be led by scholars, curators, or visiting experts.

Reference Services: Visitors have access to reference services and knowledgeable librarians who can assist with research inquiries, guiding individuals through the library's extensive holdings and helping them uncover valuable resources.

Quiet Reading Rooms: The library offers serene and elegant reading rooms where visitors can immerse themselves in scholarly pursuits. The atmosphere is conducive to focused study and contemplation.

Historical Significance: The John Hay Library has played a significant role in the academic and cultural life of Brown University and the broader community. Learning about the library's history adds depth to the tour and underscores its importance as a repository of knowledge.

A tour of the John Hay Library is a unique opportunity to step into a world of literary and historical richness. Whether you're a scholar, a history enthusiast, or someone who appreciates the beauty of rare books and manuscripts, the library provides an enriching and intellectually stimulating experience.

28. Explore the historic districts of Elmwood and South Elmwood.

Exploring the historic districts of Elmwood and South Elmwood in Providence is a journey through time, characterized by charming architecture, rich history, and vibrant community life.

Elmwood District: Elmwood is a historic neighborhood known for its diverse architecture and tree-lined streets. The district features a mix of Victorian, Colonial Revival, and other architectural styles, showcasing the evolution of residential design over the years.

Historic Homes: As you stroll through the Elmwood District, you'll encounter well-preserved historic homes, each with its unique character and charm. Many of these homes date back to the late 19th and early 20th centuries, offering a glimpse into the city's architectural heritage.

Rochambeau Avenue: Rochambeau Avenue, a prominent thoroughfare in Elmwood, is lined with historic homes and serves as a showcase for the neighborhood's architectural diversity. The wide boulevard adds to the district's aesthetic appeal.

South Elmwood: South Elmwood is an extension of Elmwood, known for its historic landmarks and community-oriented atmosphere. The district encompasses a mix of residential and commercial spaces, contributing to a lively and integrated neighborhood feel.

Broad Street: Broad Street runs through South Elmwood and is a hub of cultural diversity. The street is known for its vibrant atmosphere, diverse businesses, and a range of dining options representing different cuisines.

Knight Memorial Library: A notable landmark in Elmwood, the Knight Memorial Library is an architectural gem designed by the firm of Stone, Carpenter, and Willson. The library's distinctive Beaux-Arts style and historical significance make it a focal point in the community.

Local Businesses: Both Elmwood and South Elmwood are home to a variety of local businesses, including shops, cafes, and restaurants. Exploring these establishments allows you to experience the neighborhood's unique character and support local entrepreneurs.

Community Gardens: The Elmwood and South Elmwood districts often feature community gardens, contributing to the neighborhood's green spaces and providing residents with areas for relaxation and cultivation.

Historic Churches: The districts are home to historic churches, adding to the architectural and cultural fabric of the community. These structures often showcase distinctive design elements and serve as community landmarks.

Community Events: Elmwood and South Elmwood are known for hosting community events, fairs, and gatherings that bring residents together. These events contribute to the sense of community and provide opportunities for socializing and cultural exchange.

Exploring the historic districts of Elmwood and South Elmwood offers a delightful mix of architectural appreciation, community engagement, and a sense of the city's evolution over time. Whether you're interested in history, architecture, or simply enjoy the atmosphere of diverse and vibrant neighborhoods, these districts provide a charming and enriching experience in Providence.

29. Attend a Providence Bruins hockey game.

Attending a Providence Bruins hockey game is an exhilarating experience that combines the fast-paced action of professional hockey with the energetic atmosphere of a passionate fanbase. The Providence Bruins, the American Hockey League (AHL) affiliate of the Boston Bruins, play their home games at the Dunkin' Donuts Center in downtown Providence.

Dunkin' Donuts Center: The venue itself adds to the excitement of the game. The Dunkin' Donuts Center is a modern and well-equipped arena that provides an excellent setting for hockey enthusiasts. Its central location in downtown Providence makes it easily accessible for locals and visitors alike.

AHL Hockey: The Providence Bruins compete in the American Hockey League, which serves as the primary development league for the National Hockey League (NHL). This means that fans have the opportunity to witness emerging talent, including future NHL stars, showcasing their skills on the ice.

Fan Engagement: Providence Bruins games are known for their lively and engaged fanbase. The crowd's energy, combined with the cheers, chants, and team spirit, creates an electric atmosphere throughout the game.

Affordable Entertainment: AHL games, including Providence Bruins matches, offer an affordable and family-friendly entertainment option. Attending a game allows fans of all ages to enjoy professional hockey without the higher costs associated with NHL events.

Promotions and Giveaways: The Providence Bruins often run promotions and giveaways during their games, adding an extra layer of excitement for attendees. From themed nights to freebies for fans, these promotions enhance the overall fan experience.

Player Development: Watching a Providence Bruins game provides insight into the development of young talent within the Boston Bruins organization. Many players who have succeeded in the AHL go on to make significant contributions to the NHL team.

Community Involvement: The Providence Bruins actively engage with the local community, organizing events, and initiatives to connect with fans. This commitment to community involvement fosters a strong bond between the team and its supporters.

Concession Options: The Dunkin' Donuts Center offers a variety of concession options, allowing fans to enjoy classic game-day snacks and beverages while taking in the action on the ice.

Family-Friendly Environment: Providence Bruins games are family-friendly, making them an ideal outing for families with children. The excitement of the game, combined with the interactive and entertaining atmosphere, creates lasting memories for fans of all ages.

Whether you're a die-hard hockey fan, a casual sports enthusiast, or someone looking for an enjoyable and dynamic event in Providence, attending a Providence Bruins hockey game at the Dunkin' Donuts Center promises an unforgettable experience filled with athleticism, camaraderie, and the thrill of live hockey action.

30. Take a walk through Roger Williams National Memorial.

Taking a walk through Roger Williams National Memorial in Providence is a serene and reflective experience, offering a glimpse into the historical and cultural significance of this site dedicated to the founder of Rhode Island, Roger Williams.

Travel to Providence Rhode Island

Historical Context: Roger Williams National Memorial commemorates the life and ideals of Roger Williams, a 17th-century dissenter and advocate for religious freedom. Williams played a pivotal role in the establishment of Rhode Island as a haven for religious tolerance.

Landscape and Tranquility: The memorial is situated in a peaceful urban oasis, providing a tranquil escape from the bustling city. The carefully landscaped grounds, including walking paths and green spaces, create a contemplative environment.

Statue of Roger Williams: A prominent feature of the memorial is the statue of Roger Williams. The sculpture serves as a visual representation of the man whose beliefs in liberty and the separation of church and state left a lasting impact on the founding principles of the United States.

Educational Signage: Throughout the memorial, informative signage provides historical context and details about Roger Williams, his contributions, and the early history of Rhode Island. The site serves as an outdoor educational space, allowing visitors to learn about the roots of religious freedom in America.

Benches and Rest Areas: Benches strategically placed throughout the memorial offer opportunities for visitors to sit and reflect. The quiet surroundings make it an ideal spot for contemplation and appreciation of the natural beauty of the area.

Proximity to Waterplace Park: The memorial is conveniently located near Waterplace Park, providing an opportunity to extend the walk and enjoy the scenic views along the Providence River. Waterplace Park is known for its picturesque walking paths, bridges, and outdoor events.

Events and Programs: Roger Williams National Memorial hosts various events and programs throughout the year. These may include ranger-led walks, talks, and activities that delve deeper into the historical significance of Roger Williams and the principles he championed.

Accessibility: The memorial is designed to be accessible to visitors of all abilities, with paved paths and ramps making it easy for everyone to explore the site comfortably.

Adjacent Historic Sites: The memorial is close to other historic sites in Providence, such as the First Baptist Church in America, which is the oldest

Baptist church in the United States. Exploring the nearby historic landmarks provides a more comprehensive understanding of the city's colonial history.

Whether you're a history enthusiast, a nature lover seeking a quiet escape, or someone interested in the principles of religious freedom, a walk through Roger Williams National Memorial offers a meaningful and reflective experience in the heart of Providence.

31.Explore the Blackstone River Bikeway.

Exploring the Blackstone River Bikeway in Providence and beyond provides a scenic and recreational journey along the historic Blackstone River, offering a mix of natural beauty, cultural heritage, and outdoor activity.

Picturesque Pathways: The Blackstone River Bikeway features well-maintained and picturesque pathways that wind along the Blackstone River, providing cyclists, joggers, and walkers with a scenic route to enjoy the outdoors.

Riverside Scenery: The bikeway offers stunning views of the Blackstone River and its surrounding natural landscapes. The meandering river, tree-lined shores, and occasional wildlife sightings create a peaceful and immersive experience.

Historic Significance: The bikeway follows the route of the historic Blackstone Canal and towpath, showcasing remnants of the region's industrial past. Interpretive signs along the trail provide information about the canal's history and its role in the Industrial Revolution.

Cultural Landmarks: As you traverse the bikeway, you may encounter cultural landmarks and historical sites, including old mills, bridges, and artifacts that reflect the area's industrial heritage. These elements add depth to the journey, combining recreation with a sense of the past.

Scenic Bridges: The bikeway crosses several picturesque bridges that span the Blackstone River, offering vantage points for taking in the surrounding scenery. These bridges contribute to the charm and diversity of the route.

Multi-Use Path: The bikeway is a multi-use path that accommodates various outdoor activities. Cyclists, joggers, walkers, and even those with strollers can enjoy the well-paved and well-marked trail.

Connecting Communities: The Blackstone River Bikeway connects multiple communities along its route, providing residents and visitors with a recreational link between urban and suburban areas. This connectivity enhances the sense of community and accessibility.

Seasonal Beauty: Throughout the year, the bikeway showcases the changing seasons, with blossoming flowers in spring, vibrant foliage in fall, and serene winter landscapes. The variety of seasonal beauty adds to the allure of the trail.

Access to Parks: The bikeway passes through or is in close proximity to various parks and green spaces, providing opportunities for picnics, rest stops, and additional outdoor activities. Slater Memorial Park is one such notable park along the route.

Community Events: The Blackstone River Bikeway hosts community events, group rides, and activities that bring people together to celebrate the natural and recreational aspects of the trail. Checking local event calendars can add an extra layer of enjoyment to your visit.

Exploring the Blackstone River Bikeway offers a delightful blend of nature, history, and outdoor recreation. Whether you're seeking a leisurely stroll, an energizing bike ride, or a peaceful retreat into nature, this bikeway provides a versatile and accessible outdoor experience in the heart of Providence and beyond.

32. Attend a WaterFire Arts Center event.

Attending an event at the WaterFire Arts Center in Providence promises a unique and immersive experience, combining art, culture, and community engagement in a distinctive venue dedicated to the renowned WaterFire installations.

Architectural Gem: The WaterFire Arts Center is housed in a beautifully renovated industrial building, showcasing a blend of historic architecture and modern design. The center's adaptive reuse highlights Providence's commitment to preserving its architectural heritage.

WaterFire Installations: The Arts Center is intimately connected with the WaterFire art installations, a signature Providence event. Attending an event at the center often means being part of the larger WaterFire experience, where the rivers are illuminated with floating bonfires, accompanied by music and performances.

Gallery Spaces: The Arts Center features gallery spaces that showcase a diverse range of visual arts, including paintings, sculptures, and multimedia installations. The exhibitions provide a platform for local and international artists, contributing to Providence's vibrant arts scene.

Performance Spaces: The venue hosts various performing arts events, including theater productions, dance performances, and live music. These events add to the cultural richness of the space, offering attendees a dynamic and engaging experience.

Educational Programs: The WaterFire Arts Center is committed to education and community outreach. Events may include workshops, lectures, and educational programs that promote artistic learning and creativity for people of all ages.

Culinary Experiences: Some events at the Arts Center incorporate culinary experiences, such as tastings, food pairings, or collaborations with local chefs. These elements enhance the overall sensory experience for attendees.

Community Engagement: The center serves as a hub for community engagement, fostering connections between artists, residents, and visitors. Events often bring diverse groups of people together to celebrate art and culture.

Special Events: The WaterFire Arts Center hosts special events throughout the year, such as art openings, fundraisers, and celebrations tied to the WaterFire installations. These events contribute to the festive and inclusive atmosphere of the center.

Outdoor Spaces: The Arts Center includes outdoor spaces that can be utilized for events, gatherings, and performances. These spaces take advantage of the center's location along the Woonasquatucket River and add to the versatility of the venue.

Waterfront Setting: The center's location near the waterfront provides a scenic backdrop for events. Attendees can enjoy views of the river and surrounding landscapes, creating a picturesque setting for cultural and artistic experiences.

Travel to Providence Rhode Island

Attending an event at the WaterFire Arts Center is more than just a cultural outing; it's an immersion into the artistic spirit of Providence. Whether you're drawn to visual arts, performances, or the unique ambiance created by WaterFire installations, the Arts Center offers a dynamic and enriching cultural experience in the heart of the city.

33. Take a boat tour of Narragansett Bay.

Embarking on a boat tour of Narragansett Bay in Providence offers a captivating maritime experience, allowing you to explore the bay's scenic beauty, historic landmarks, and coastal charm. Here's what you might encounter during this nautical adventure:

Panoramic Views: A boat tour provides breathtaking panoramic views of Narragansett Bay, showcasing the beauty of the coastline, the shimmering water, and the surrounding landscapes. The vantage point from the water offers a unique and picturesque perspective.

Historic Landmarks: Narragansett Bay is rich in history, and a boat tour often includes commentary on the historical significance of landmarks along the shoreline. You might pass by lighthouses, forts, and other structures that tell the story of the region's maritime past.

Newport Harbor: Depending on the tour route, you may have the opportunity to explore Newport Harbor. This historic harbor is renowned for its maritime heritage, upscale yachting culture, and views of iconic mansions along the shoreline.

Marine Wildlife: Narragansett Bay is home to diverse marine life. During the boat tour, you might spot seabirds, seals, and other wildlife. The narrated tour may provide insights into the local ecosystem and the importance of preserving these natural habitats.

Sailing Excursions: Some boat tours offer the chance to experience the bay on a sailing vessel. Whether it's a classic schooner or a modern sailboat, the serenity of sailing adds to the overall enjoyment of the journey.

Spectacular Sunsets: Sunset boat tours are a popular option, allowing you to witness the bay's transformation as the sun dips below the horizon. The warm hues reflecting off the water create a magical and romantic atmosphere.

Aquidneck Island: Narragansett Bay surrounds Aquidneck Island, home to towns like Newport and Portsmouth. Boat tours may provide glimpses of these charming coastal communities and their historic architecture.

Themed Tours: Some boat tours are themed, focusing on specific aspects of the bay's history, ecology, or cultural significance. These themed tours offer a more in-depth exploration of particular interests.

Private Charters: For a more personalized experience, private boat charters are often available. Whether for a special occasion or an intimate gathering, a private charter allows you to customize the tour to suit your preferences.

Relaxation and Recreation: Beyond the educational and scenic aspects, a boat tour offers a leisurely and relaxing experience. The gentle rocking of the boat, the fresh sea breeze, and the sounds of the water contribute to a tranquil and enjoyable outing.

A boat tour of Narragansett Bay provides a wonderful blend of natural beauty, maritime history, and recreational enjoyment. Whether you're a history buff, nature enthusiast, or someone seeking a peaceful escape on the water, this nautical adventure offers a memorable exploration of one of Rhode Island's most iconic and picturesque locations.

34. Visit the Museum of Work and Culture in Woonsocket.

Visiting the Museum of Work and Culture in Woonsocket, Rhode Island, is a journey into the history of industrialization, labor, and the vibrant cultural tapestry of the Blackstone Valley. Here's what you might experience during your visit:

Industrial Heritage: The Museum of Work and Culture is dedicated to preserving and showcasing the industrial heritage of the Blackstone Valley. Exhibits delve into the region's transformation from a rural, agrarian landscape to a center of industrial innovation during the 19th and early 20th centuries.

Textile Industry: Woonsocket played a significant role in the American textile industry, and the museum explores this history in depth. Exhibits may include artifacts, machinery, and interactive displays that highlight the evolution of textile manufacturing and its impact on the community.

Immigrant Stories: The museum emphasizes the stories of the diverse immigrant communities that settled in the Blackstone Valley to work in the mills. Personal narratives, photographs, and cultural artifacts provide insights into the experiences of French-Canadian, Irish, and other immigrant groups.

Multimedia Presentations: Modern exhibits often incorporate multimedia elements, such as audiovisual presentations and interactive displays. These technologies enhance the visitor experience, offering a dynamic and engaging way to learn about the past.

Cultural Celebrations: The museum may host events and celebrations that showcase the rich cultural traditions of the immigrant communities that shaped the region. These events provide a lively and immersive experience for visitors.

Architectural Context: Housed in the former Social Hall of the Woonsocket YMCA, the museum's location itself is a piece of history. The building's architecture and layout may reflect the social and recreational aspects of community life during the industrial era.

Educational Programs: The museum often offers educational programs for visitors of all ages. These programs may include guided tours, workshops, and outreach initiatives that aim to educate the public about the significance of the region's industrial and cultural history.

Temporary Exhibits: In addition to its permanent exhibits, the museum frequently features temporary exhibits that delve into specific aspects of the Blackstone Valley's history, culture, or contemporary issues.

Gift Shop: Many museums have a gift shop that offers books, souvenirs, and crafts related to the exhibits. It's an opportunity to take home a memento or dive deeper into the history through literature.

Community Engagement: The Museum of Work and Culture actively engages with the local community. This might include partnerships with schools, collaborations with local organizations, and participation in community events.

By visiting the Museum of Work and Culture in Woonsocket, you have the chance to explore the dynamic history of labor, industry, and immigration that shaped the Blackstone Valley. It's a cultural and educational experience that sheds light on the resilience and diversity of the communities that contributed to the region's industrial legacy.

35. Explore the Providence Ghost Tour.

Embarking on the Providence Ghost Tour is a thrilling and eerie adventure that takes you through the historic streets of Providence, unraveling tales of paranormal activity, haunted locations, and the city's mysterious past. Here's what you might encounter during this haunting exploration:

Historic Districts: The Providence Ghost Tour typically guides participants through historic districts, such as Benefit Street and College Hill, where centuries-old architecture sets the stage for ghostly tales. These areas are known for their rich history and rumored paranormal occurrences.

Costumed Guides: Your journey is led by knowledgeable and engaging guides, often dressed in period costumes. These guides skillfully blend historical facts with ghost stories, creating a captivating and immersive experience.

Haunted Locations: The tour visits reputedly haunted locations with ties to Providence's history. Whether it's a colonial-era home, a centuries-old cemetery, or a mysterious alley, each site has its own ghostly lore waiting to be shared.

Ghost Stories: Throughout the tour, guides recount chilling ghost stories and legends associated with the locations you visit. These tales may involve historical figures, tragic events, or supernatural occurrences that have become part of Providence's spectral lore.

Nighttime Atmosphere: The Providence Ghost Tour typically takes place in the evening, adding to the eerie ambiance. As darkness falls, the historic streets and dimly lit sites contribute to the spine-tingling atmosphere of the experience.

Historical Context: In addition to ghostly tales, the tour provides historical context about Providence, shedding light on the city's past, notable residents, and significant events. This combination of history and ghost lore adds depth to the narrative.

Interactive Elements: Some ghost tours incorporate interactive elements, allowing participants to use paranormal investigation tools or engage in activities that heighten the suspense. These experiences add an extra layer of excitement to the tour.

Local Legends: Beyond documented hauntings, the tour may explore local urban legends and folklore. These stories contribute to the tapestry of supernatural tales woven into Providence's cultural heritage.

Group Dynamics: The tour often creates a sense of camaraderie among participants as you share in the spine-chilling experience. Group dynamics and shared reactions enhance the overall enjoyment of the tour.

Seasonal Variations: Depending on the time of year, the Providence Ghost Tour might offer special editions tied to Halloween or other seasonal themes. These variations can provide a unique and immersive experience based on the time of your visit.

Embarking on the Providence Ghost Tour is not just about seeking scares; it's an opportunity to delve into the mysterious and spectral side of the city's history. Whether you're a skeptic or a believer, the tour offers a captivating blend of storytelling, local history, and the thrill of the unknown as you explore the haunted corners of Providence.

36. Attend a performance by the Rhode Island Philharmonic Orchestra.

Attending a performance by the Rhode Island Philharmonic Orchestra is a cultural and auditory treat, offering a world-class musical experience in Providence. Here's what you might experience during your visit:

Acclaimed Venue: Performances by the Rhode Island Philharmonic Orchestra often take place at prestigious venues such as The VETS (Veterans Memorial Auditorium) or other concert halls in the area. These venues are known for their acoustics and provide an elegant setting for classical music performances.

Orchestral Excellence: The Rhode Island Philharmonic Orchestra is composed of highly skilled musicians, including talented instrumentalists and a conductor. The orchestra's commitment to musical excellence ensures a captivating and nuanced performance.

Diverse Repertoire: The orchestra's repertoire spans a wide range of musical genres and styles. From classical masterpieces to contemporary compositions, each performance showcases the versatility and artistry of the ensemble.

Guest Soloists: Depending on the program, the orchestra may feature guest soloists—renowned instrumentalists or vocalists who collaborate with the ensemble. These solo performances add an extra layer of virtuosity and variety to the concert.

Conductor's Interpretation: The role of the conductor is pivotal in shaping the orchestra's interpretation of the music. The conductor's vision and direction contribute to the overall emotional impact and coherence of the performance.

Seasonal Concert Series: The Rhode Island Philharmonic Orchestra typically offers a seasonal concert series, featuring performances throughout the year. Seasonal variations may include themed concerts, holiday performances, and collaborative events with other artistic organizations.

Educational Initiatives: The orchestra is often engaged in educational initiatives, reaching out to schools and the community to promote music education. Some performances may include special programs or collaborations aimed at fostering an appreciation for classical music among diverse audiences.

Cultural Enrichment: Attending a performance by the Rhode Island Philharmonic Orchestra provides cultural enrichment, exposing audiences to the timeless beauty of orchestral music. The experience goes beyond entertainment, offering a profound connection to the arts.

Subscription Packages: Patrons often have the option to purchase subscription packages for the entire concert season. Subscribers enjoy benefits such as priority seating, exclusive events, and a curated series of performances.

Community Engagement: The orchestra actively engages with the local community through outreach programs, open rehearsals, and events designed to make classical music accessible to a broad audience. This community engagement fosters a connection between the orchestra and its supporters.

Whether you're a seasoned classical music enthusiast or someone looking to explore the world of orchestral performances, attending a concert by the Rhode Island Philharmonic Orchestra promises an enriching and memorable experience, celebrating the timeless beauty of live symphonic music.

37. Take a cooking class at a local culinary school.

Participating in a cooking class at a local culinary school in Providence is an immersive and enjoyable experience, offering hands-on culinary education, expert guidance, and the opportunity to enhance your culinary skills. Here's what you might expect during your cooking class:

Expert Instruction: Culinary schools often have skilled and experienced chefs as instructors. These professionals provide expert guidance, sharing their knowledge, techniques, and culinary tips throughout the class.

Hands-On Learning: Cooking classes are typically hands-on, allowing participants to actively engage in the preparation of dishes. This hands-on approach ensures that you not only learn theory but also gain practical experience in the kitchen.

Varied Themes and Cuisines: Culinary schools often offer classes with diverse themes and cuisines. Whether you're interested in mastering a specific cooking technique, exploring international cuisines, or learning to prepare a particular type of dish, there's likely a class to suit your culinary interests.

High-Quality Ingredients: Classes at culinary schools often use high-quality, fresh ingredients. This emphasis on quality ensures that participants experience cooking with the best possible elements, contributing to the overall enjoyment of the culinary process.

State-of-the-Art Facilities: Culinary schools typically have well-equipped kitchens with modern appliances and tools. Participants have the opportunity to work in a professional kitchen environment, enhancing their cooking skills using industry-standard equipment.

Recipe Demos and Tastings: In addition to hands-on cooking, instructors may provide recipe demonstrations, explaining techniques and offering insights into the science of cooking. Tastings are often part of the experience, allowing participants to savor the fruits of their labor.

Small Class Sizes: To facilitate personalized instruction, culinary schools often keep class sizes small. This ensures that participants receive individual attention, have their questions addressed, and can actively participate in the cooking process.

Social Experience: Cooking classes provide a social setting where participants can interact with each other, share their culinary experiences, and enjoy the camaraderie of fellow food enthusiasts. It's an opportunity to connect with like-minded individuals in a fun and relaxed environment.

Takeaway Recipes: Participants typically receive copies of the recipes used in the class. This allows you to recreate the dishes at home, reinforcing the skills and techniques learned during the class.

Gift Opportunities: Cooking classes make for excellent gifts. Many culinary schools offer gift certificates or specific classes tailored for gift-giving occasions, making it a thoughtful and experiential present for friends and family.

Whether you're a novice in the kitchen or an experienced home cook looking to expand your culinary repertoire, taking a cooking class at a local culinary school in Providence offers a delightful and educational experience that combines the joy of cooking with the art of gastronomy.

38. Attend a film screening at the Providence French Film Festival.

Attending a film screening at the Providence French Film Festival is a cultural and cinematic experience that brings the best of French cinema to the heart of Providence. Here's what you might encounter during your visit to the festival:

Diverse Film Selection: The Providence French Film Festival typically showcases a diverse selection of French films, including feature films, documentaries, and shorts. The curated lineup often represents a mix of genres, styles, and themes, providing a comprehensive overview of contemporary French cinema.

International and Independent Films: The festival may feature both widely acclaimed films from established directors and independent gems that offer unique perspectives and storytelling approaches. This diversity adds richness to the cinematic experience.

Travel to Providence Rhode Island

Cultural Immersion: French cinema often reflects the cultural nuances and societal issues of France. Attending the festival provides an opportunity to immerse yourself in French culture, language, and artistic expression.

Venue Atmosphere: Film screenings at the festival are typically held in atmospheric venues, such as theaters or cultural spaces that enhance the overall cinematic experience. The ambiance contributes to the enjoyment of the films.

Q&A Sessions and Filmmaker Interactions: Some screenings may include Q&A sessions with filmmakers, directors, or other industry professionals. This interactive element allows audiences to gain insights into the creative process, inspirations behind the films, and the filmmaking industry.

Subtitles: For those not fluent in French, films are often screened with English subtitles, ensuring accessibility for a diverse audience. This allows attendees to fully appreciate the dialogue and nuances of the storytelling.

Cinematic Appreciation: The festival provides a platform for cinematic appreciation, allowing film enthusiasts to discover new works, engage in discussions about filmmaking, and expand their understanding of the art form.

Thematic Programming: Some festivals organize thematic programming, focusing on specific genres, movements, or cultural aspects within French cinema. This approach offers a more curated and in-depth exploration of the cinematic landscape.

Networking Opportunities: Film festivals often attract a mix of film professionals, enthusiasts, and industry insiders. Attending the Providence French Film Festival provides networking opportunities for those interested in the world of cinema.

Community Engagement: The festival contributes to community engagement by bringing people together to celebrate the art of filmmaking. It fosters a shared appreciation for French cinema and provides a platform for cultural exchange.

Whether you're a cinephile with a passion for French cinema or someone looking to explore international films, attending a screening at the Providence French Film Festival offers a unique and enriching experience. It's a celebration of storytelling, artistic expression, and the global language of cinema in the vibrant cultural landscape of Providence.

39. Explore the Ladd Observatory.

Exploring the Ladd Observatory in Providence is a fascinating journey into astronomy, celestial observation, and historical preservation. Here's what you might experience during your visit:

Historical Significance: The Ladd Observatory, located on the grounds of Brown University, has a rich history dating back to its establishment in 1891. Its historical significance lies in its role as a research and teaching facility and its contributions to the field of astronomy.

Architectural Charm: The observatory building itself is a charming example of late 19th-century architecture. Its unique design and observatory dome contribute to the aesthetic appeal of the site.

Telescopes and Instruments: The Ladd Observatory houses several telescopes and observational instruments. While the technology has evolved over the years, some historic telescopes may still be in use. Visitors may have the opportunity to view celestial objects through these instruments.

Public Open Nights: The observatory often hosts public open nights, allowing visitors to peer through telescopes and observe the night sky. These events provide an educational and interactive experience for individuals of all ages.

Stargazing Sessions: Depending on the schedule and weather conditions, the observatory may organize stargazing sessions. This allows visitors to learn about different celestial objects, constellations, and astronomical phenomena from knowledgeable guides.

Educational Programs: The Ladd Observatory is actively involved in educational outreach. Programs may include astronomy lectures, workshops, and educational initiatives aimed at schools and community groups.

Astronomical Exhibits: The observatory may feature exhibits that provide insights into the history of astronomy, notable discoveries, and the role of the Ladd Observatory in advancing astronomical knowledge.

Astronomy Library: Some observatories, including Ladd, have libraries with a collection of astronomical literature. Visitors may have access to resources that delve into various aspects of astronomy and astrophysics.

Travel to Providence Rhode Island

Community Engagement: The observatory serves as a hub for community engagement in the realm of astronomy. Whether through public events, educational programs, or collaborative initiatives, it fosters a sense of curiosity and exploration.

Dark Sky Site: The location of the Ladd Observatory may contribute to its suitability as a dark sky site. This designation ensures minimal light pollution, providing optimal conditions for stargazing and celestial observation.

Visiting the Ladd Observatory offers a blend of historical appreciation, astronomical education, and the thrill of stargazing. Whether you're a seasoned astronomer or someone curious about the mysteries of the universe, the observatory provides a unique and enriching experience within the academic and scientific landscape of Brown University in Providence.

40. Visit the Sprout CoWorking Art Gallery.

Visiting the Sprout CoWorking Art Gallery in Providence promises a vibrant and dynamic experience, combining coworking spaces with a showcase of local artistic talent. Here's what you might encounter during your visit:

Artistic Workspace: Sprout CoWorking is known for providing coworking spaces that blend professional work environments with a creative and artistic ambiance. The art gallery is an extension of this ethos, creating a space where art and work intersect.

Local Artist Exhibitions: The gallery regularly features exhibitions by local artists. These exhibitions showcase a diverse range of artistic styles, mediums, and themes, offering a platform for emerging and established artists in the Providence community.

Rotating Art Displays: The gallery likely has a rotating schedule of art displays, ensuring that each visit may reveal new and exciting artworks. This dynamic approach keeps the space fresh and continuously introduces visitors to a variety of artistic expressions.

Multidisciplinary Art: Sprout CoWorking Art Gallery may embrace a multidisciplinary approach to art. Expect to see paintings, sculptures, photography, and possibly even interactive or multimedia installations that contribute to the gallery's eclectic atmosphere.

Community Engagement: The gallery serves as a focal point for community engagement, bringing together artists, professionals, and art enthusiasts. Events, openings, and art-related activities may foster a sense of connection and collaboration within the local creative community.

Accessibility: One of the strengths of coworking spaces with art galleries is their accessibility. The combination of workspace and art allows professionals to engage with art during their workday, providing a source of inspiration and creativity in a professional setting.

Gallery Events: Sprout CoWorking Art Gallery may host special events such as art receptions, artist talks, and workshops. These events provide opportunities for the public to interact with artists, gain insights into the creative process, and deepen their appreciation for art.

Art for Purchase: Some artworks displayed in the gallery may be available for purchase. This arrangement not only supports local artists but also allows visitors to bring a piece of the vibrant local art scene into their homes or workspaces.

Collaborations with Local Organizations: The gallery might collaborate with other local organizations, art collectives, or initiatives. These collaborations contribute to the gallery's role as a hub for artistic and cultural exchange within Providence.

Integration with Coworking Experience: The integration of the art gallery with the coworking space creates a unique environment where professionals can work in an inspiring setting surrounded by curated art. This integration may enhance the overall experience for both artists and those utilizing the coworking facilities.

By visiting the Sprout CoWorking Art Gallery, you not only get a glimpse into the local art scene but also experience the synergy of art and work within a collaborative and creative environment. Whether you're a professional seeking an inspiring workspace or an art enthusiast exploring the local art scene, the gallery at Sprout CoWorking provides a dynamic and engaging space in the heart of Providence.

Travel to Providence Rhode Island

41. Attend a poetry reading at a local cafe.

Attending a poetry reading at a local café in Providence is a wonderful way to immerse yourself in the literary and artistic community. Here's what you might experience during your visit:

Intimate Setting: Local cafés often provide an intimate and cozy setting for poetry readings. The relaxed atmosphere allows for a more personal and engaging experience between poets and the audience.

Local Poets: Poetry readings frequently feature local poets, providing a platform for emerging and established literary voices within the community. This creates a sense of connection and support for the vibrant local arts scene.

Diverse Styles and Themes: Poetry readings showcase a diverse range of poetic styles, themes, and voices. From traditional forms to contemporary spoken word, you can expect a rich tapestry of expression that reflects the diverse perspectives of the poets.

Open Mic Opportunities: Some poetry readings include open mic sessions, allowing aspiring poets or members of the audience to share their own work. This interactive element fosters community engagement and encourages a sense of inclusivity.

Cultural Exchange: Poetry readings often touch upon various cultural and societal themes. The exploration of diverse perspectives and experiences adds a layer of cultural exchange, providing attendees with insights into different aspects of the human experience.

Live Performance: Poetry is inherently a live art form, and attending a reading allows you to experience the nuances of language, rhythm, and emotion as conveyed by the poets themselves. The live performance aspect adds a unique dimension to the appreciation of poetry.

Coffeehouse Vibe: The café setting contributes to the overall ambiance of the event. Sipping on a cup of coffee or tea while listening to poetry creates a cozy and casual atmosphere, perfect for fostering conversation and reflection.

Audience Interaction: Poetry readings often involve interaction between poets and the audience. Q&A sessions, discussions about the creative process, and reflections on the themes explored in the poetry contribute to a dynamic and participatory experience.

Promotion of Local Arts: Café poetry readings support and promote the local arts scene. They provide a platform for poets to share their work, connect with the community, and contribute to the cultural richness of Providence.

Event Series: Some cafés host regular poetry reading events or series. If you find a reading you enjoy, it's likely that the café regularly curates literary events, providing ongoing opportunities to engage with poetry and the local literary community.

Attending a poetry reading at a local café offers a delightful blend of artistic expression, community connection, and the simple pleasures of enjoying good poetry in a cozy setting. It's a chance to experience the power of words and creativity within the warm and inviting atmosphere of a Providence café.

42. Take a tour of the historic Fox Point neighborhood.

Taking a tour of the historic Fox Point neighborhood in Providence offers a journey through time, exploring its rich history, diverse architecture, and cultural heritage. Here's what you might encounter during your visit:

Colonial Roots: Fox Point traces its roots back to the colonial era. The neighborhood was settled in the 17th century, and remnants of its early history can still be seen in the layout and architecture of certain buildings.

Fox Point Hurricane Barrier: One of the notable features of the neighborhood is the Fox Point Hurricane Barrier, a structure designed to protect the area from storm surges. This engineering marvel showcases the city's response to natural challenges.

Historic Homes: Fox Point is home to a variety of historic houses, ranging from colonial and Federal-style homes to later Victorian and Queen Anne-style residences. Walking through the streets allows you to appreciate the architectural evolution of the neighborhood.

India Point Park: Located along the waterfront, India Point Park is a scenic spot where you can enjoy views of the Seekonk River. The park is often used for

Travel to Providence Rhode Island

recreational activities, events, and offers a pleasant green space within the urban setting.

Historic Churches: Fox Point boasts several historic churches, each with its own architectural and historical significance. These include structures like St. John's Church, adding to the neighborhood's cultural and religious diversity.

Cultural Diversity: Over the years, Fox Point has been shaped by waves of immigration, contributing to its cultural diversity. You might find evidence of this diversity in local businesses, restaurants, and cultural institutions within the neighborhood.

Wickenden Street: Wickenden Street is a bustling commercial district in Fox Point known for its eclectic mix of shops, restaurants, and cafes. The street exudes a vibrant and artsy atmosphere, making it a popular destination for locals and visitors alike.

Providence River Walk: The Providence River Walk extends through Fox Point, providing a picturesque path along the waterfront. It's a great way to explore the neighborhood on foot, with opportunities to discover public art and enjoy the riverside scenery.

Brown University Influence: Fox Point is located near Brown University, and the influence of the university is felt in the neighborhood. Some historic homes may have connections to the university's early years.

Neighborhood Events: Fox Point often hosts neighborhood events, festivals, and gatherings. These events showcase the community spirit and provide opportunities for residents and visitors to come together.

Culinary Delights: The neighborhood is known for its diverse culinary scene. From charming cafes to international cuisine, Fox Point offers a range of dining options that reflect its eclectic character.

Exploring the historic Fox Point neighborhood is like stepping into a living history book. It's a neighborhood that has evolved over centuries, and each corner tells a story of the people, events, and architectural styles that have shaped its character. Whether you're interested in history, architecture, or simply enjoying the vibrant atmosphere of a diverse neighborhood, Fox Point has something to offer.

43. Explore the Providence Art Club.

Exploring the Providence Art Club provides a unique opportunity to immerse yourself in the local art scene and appreciate the works of talented artists. Here's what you might experience during your visit:

Historic Significance: Founded in 1880, the Providence Art Club is one of the oldest art clubs in the United States. Its historic significance adds a layer of cultural richness to the art community in Providence.

Clubhouse and Galleries: The Providence Art Club is housed in a charming historic building. The clubhouse itself is an architectural gem and serves as a venue for various art exhibitions, showcasing the works of both members and guest artists.

Rotating Exhibitions: The club's galleries host rotating exhibitions throughout the year. These exhibitions feature a diverse range of artistic styles, mediums, and themes, reflecting the dynamic and ever-evolving nature of the local art scene.

Member Artists: The Providence Art Club is home to a community of member artists. Exploring the galleries allows you to appreciate the talent and creativity of these local artists, many of whom may have achieved recognition for their contributions to the art world.

Art Sales and Collections: Some exhibitions may offer works for sale, providing visitors with the opportunity to support local artists and add unique pieces to their art collections. The club's collection itself may include notable pieces acquired over its long history.

Open Studios and Workshops: The Providence Art Club often organizes open studio events and workshops, providing a behind-the-scenes look at the artistic process. Attendees may have the chance to interact with artists, ask questions, and gain insights into different artistic techniques.

Culinary and Social Events: Beyond the art exhibitions, the Providence Art Club occasionally hosts culinary and social events. These events create a vibrant and inclusive atmosphere, fostering connections among artists and art enthusiasts.

Membership Opportunities: The club offers membership opportunities for artists and art lovers alike. Becoming a member allows individuals to actively participate in the club's activities, gain access to special events, and contribute to the local art community.

Landscape Painting at The Shady Lea School: The Providence Art Club operates a satellite location, the Shady Lea School in North Kingstown, where members can participate in landscape painting sessions. This adds a plein air aspect to the club's activities.

Historical Tours: The historic clubhouse itself is a point of interest. Guided tours may provide insights into the history of the building, its architectural features, and the role it has played in the cultural life of Providence.

Exploring the Providence Art Club offers a multifaceted experience—immersing you in the visual arts, connecting you with local artists, and providing a glimpse into the cultural heritage of Providence. Whether you're an art enthusiast, a collector, or someone interested in the creative process, the Providence Art Club is a gem within the city's artistic landscape.

44. Attend a WaterFire Full Lighting ceremony.

Attending a WaterFire Full Lighting ceremony in Providence is a captivating and enchanting experience that combines art, culture, and community. Here's what you might encounter during your visit:

Symbolic Lighting of the River: WaterFire is an art installation that features the lighting of a series of bonfires along the waterways of downtown Providence. The fires are set afloat on braziers, creating a mesmerizing spectacle that illuminates the rivers and bridges.

Awe-Inspiring Atmosphere: As the sun sets and darkness falls, the fires are lit, transforming the urban landscape into a magical and otherworldly scene. The warm glow of the flames reflects on the water, creating a truly enchanting atmosphere.

Artistic Installations: WaterFire is not just about fire; it's a holistic art installation. The experience includes floating sculptures, ambient music, and other artistic elements that contribute to the immersive and sensory-rich environment.

Community Gathering: WaterFire events draw a diverse crowd of locals and visitors. The installations are often accompanied by live music, creating a communal gathering space where people come together to share in the experience.

Boat Processions: Some WaterFire events feature boat processions, adding an extra layer of visual interest. Boats carrying performers or dignitaries may traverse the waterways, creating a dynamic element to the overall presentation.

Ritualistic Ceremonies: WaterFire is often accompanied by ritualistic ceremonies and performances that add cultural and symbolic depth to the event. These ceremonies may include fire dancers, torchbearers, or other performances that enhance the overall narrative.

Bridge of Stars: The event may include a "Bridge of Stars" where luminaria bags line the bridges, creating a celestial pathway over the water. This feature adds to the ethereal and dreamlike quality of the installation.

Volunteer Involvement: WaterFire is a community-driven event that relies heavily on volunteers. From the lighting of the fires to organizing logistics, volunteers play a crucial role in bringing this unique experience to life.

Seasonal Themes: WaterFire events may be organized around specific themes, tying into cultural or seasonal celebrations. These themes can influence the artistic elements, performances, and overall ambiance of the event.

Nighttime Markets: In conjunction with WaterFire, there may be nighttime markets or food vendors along the riverbanks. This allows attendees to indulge in local cuisine and artisanal products while enjoying the event.

Impact on Local Businesses: WaterFire has a positive impact on local businesses, attracting visitors to the city and contributing to the economic vitality of the downtown area.

Attending a WaterFire Full Lighting ceremony is not just a visual spectacle but an immersive and communal experience that engages the senses and fosters a sense of shared wonder. It's a testament to the power of art to transform urban spaces and create a magical and memorable atmosphere for all who participate.

Travel to Providence Rhode Island

45. Take a Providence Riverboat Company cruise.

Embarking on a Providence Riverboat Company cruise is a delightful way to explore the waterways of Providence and appreciate the city's scenic beauty. Here's what you might experience during your riverboat cruise:

Scenic Waterways: The cruise takes you along the picturesque waterways of Providence, offering panoramic views of the city skyline, historic architecture, and natural landscapes. The vantage point from the water provides a unique perspective of the city.

Knowledgeable Guides: Riverboat tours typically come with knowledgeable guides who share interesting facts, historical anecdotes, and information about the landmarks and points of interest along the route. Their commentary enhances your understanding of Providence's rich history and culture.

Landmarks and Architecture: The cruise may pass by notable landmarks and architectural gems, such as the Rhode Island State House, Waterplace Park, College Hill, and other iconic structures. This allows you to appreciate the city's diverse architectural styles and historical significance.

WaterFire Perspectives: If you take an evening cruise during a WaterFire event, you'll have the opportunity to witness the magical ambiance of the fires reflecting on the water. The combination of the riverboat cruise and WaterFire creates a captivating experience.

Relaxing Atmosphere: Riverboat cruises offer a leisurely and relaxing atmosphere. Whether you're seated on the deck or in a comfortable cabin, you can unwind, enjoy the gentle breeze, and take in the scenic surroundings.

Educational Experience: In addition to narrated tours, some riverboat cruises may offer educational programs or themed cruises that focus on specific aspects of Providence's history, culture, or ecology. These experiences add depth to your understanding of the city.

Wildlife Observation: Cruises along the waterways may provide opportunities for wildlife observation. Keep an eye out for birds, marine life, and other natural elements that contribute to the ecological diversity of the area.

Sunset Cruises: Consider taking a sunset cruise for a romantic and visually stunning experience. Watching the sun dip below the horizon while gliding along the water creates a memorable and picturesque scene.

Private Charters: Some riverboat companies offer private charters for special events, celebrations, or group outings. This option allows you to customize the experience and enjoy a more intimate setting with your companions.

Photography Opportunities: The cruise provides ample opportunities for photography enthusiasts to capture scenic views, cityscapes, and waterfront landscapes. The changing light throughout the day adds to the photographic appeal.

Seasonal Events: Riverboat companies may organize cruises tied to seasonal events or festivals. Whether it's a fall foliage cruise, a summer celebration, or a holiday-themed cruise, these special events offer a festive and enjoyable experience.

A Providence Riverboat Company cruise is not just a journey along the water; it's an immersive and scenic adventure that connects you with the city's history, culture, and natural beauty. Whether you're a local resident or a visitor, the cruise provides a unique perspective on Providence, creating memories that linger long after the voyage concludes.

46. Attend a play at the Wilbury Theatre Group.

Attending a play at the Wilbury Theatre Group in Providence promises a captivating and immersive theatrical experience. Here's what you might encounter during your visit:

Innovative Productions: The Wilbury Theatre Group is known for its commitment to producing innovative and thought-provoking theatrical works. Productions often explore contemporary themes, pushing the boundaries of traditional storytelling.

Intimate Venue: The theater group operates in an intimate venue, creating a close connection between the performers and the audience. This setting allows for a more immersive and engaging theatrical experience.

Travel to Providence Rhode Island

Diverse Range of Plays: The Wilbury Theatre Group curates a diverse repertoire of plays, including classics, new works, and experimental pieces. This variety caters to different tastes and provides an opportunity to discover unique and cutting-edge performances.

Local and Guest Artists: The group collaborates with both local and guest artists, bringing a mix of talents to the stage. This contributes to the dynamic and inclusive nature of the theater community in Providence.

Inclusive Programming: Wilbury Theatre Group is known for its commitment to inclusivity. The programming often reflects a dedication to diversity, equity, and inclusion, both on and off the stage.

Thematic Explorations: Productions at Wilbury often delve into complex themes, social issues, and contemporary topics. The plays may provoke thought, spark conversations, and provide a platform for exploring different perspectives.

Emerging Artists: The theater group actively supports emerging artists, providing a platform for new talent to showcase their skills. This commitment to fostering the next generation of theater-makers adds vibrancy to the local arts scene.

Post-Show Discussions: Some productions may include post-show discussions or talkbacks, allowing the audience to engage with the artists and delve deeper into the themes explored in the play. This interactive element enhances the overall theater-going experience.

Seasonal Themes: The theater group often organizes its programming around thematic seasons, creating a cohesive and curated experience for the audience. Seasonal themes may tie together a series of plays that explore interconnected ideas.

Community Engagement: Wilbury Theatre Group is actively involved in community engagement initiatives. This may include educational programs, outreach to schools, and collaborative projects that connect the arts with the local community.

Artistic Collaborations: The theater group may collaborate with other artistic organizations, fostering cross-disciplinary projects that integrate theater with other forms of artistic expression.

Accessible Performances: Efforts are often made to ensure that performances are accessible to diverse audiences. This may include offering discounted tickets, providing subtitles or sign language interpreters, and creating a welcoming environment for all patrons.

Attending a play at the Wilbury Theatre Group is not just about witnessing a performance; it's an opportunity to engage with thought-provoking art, support local and emerging talent, and become part of a community that values the transformative power of theater. The experience is sure to leave a lasting impression and ignite a passion for the performing arts.

47. Explore the Wanskuck Historic District.

Exploring the Wanskuck Historic District in Providence offers a glimpse into the area's industrial past and the preservation of its historical character. Here's what you might encounter during your visit:

Industrial Heritage: Wanskuck was historically an industrial area, known for its mills and manufacturing activities during the 19th and early 20th centuries. The district retains remnants of this industrial heritage in its architecture and landscape.

Historic Mills: You may come across historic mill buildings that once played a crucial role in the textile and manufacturing industries. These structures stand as tangible reminders of Wanskuck's industrial history.

Residential Architecture: The district is characterized by a mix of residential architecture, showcasing styles from different periods. You might find examples of Victorian, Colonial Revival, and other architectural styles that reflect the evolution of the neighborhood.

Wanskuck Library: The Wanskuck Library, a Carnegie library built in the early 20th century, is a notable landmark in the district. Carnegie libraries were funded by philanthropist Andrew Carnegie, and this one serves as a testament to the importance of education in the community.

Neighborhood Parks: Wanskuck features neighborhood parks and green spaces where you can enjoy a leisurely stroll or take in the surroundings. These spaces provide a tranquil contrast to the industrial history of the district.

Community Character: The district has maintained a strong sense of community character. The residential areas are often interspersed with small businesses, local shops, and community gathering spaces that contribute to the neighborhood's identity.

Preservation Efforts: Efforts to preserve the historic character of Wanskuck can be observed in the conservation of buildings and public spaces. This commitment to preservation helps ensure that future generations can appreciate the district's rich history.

Local Businesses: Explore local businesses and shops that add to the vibrancy of the neighborhood. You might find establishments that have been part of the community for years, contributing to the sense of continuity and local identity.

Walkable Streets: The layout of Wanskuck includes walkable streets that invite residents and visitors to explore the district on foot. Walking through the neighborhood allows you to appreciate the details of the historic architecture and absorb the ambiance of the area.

Cultural Diversity: Like many neighborhoods in Providence, Wanskuck reflects the city's cultural diversity. The mix of residential and commercial spaces creates an environment where different cultures and communities coexist.

Public Art: Keep an eye out for public art installations that may enhance the aesthetic appeal of the district. Public art often contributes to the sense of place and community pride.

Exploring the Wanskuck Historic District offers a multifaceted experience—connecting you with the industrial roots of Providence, showcasing architectural diversity, and immersing you in the daily life and community spirit of this historically significant neighborhood.

48.Attend the Rhode Island International Film Festival.

Attending the Rhode Island International Film Festival (RIIFF) is an exciting and enriching experience, offering a showcase of diverse and compelling films from around the world. Here's what you might encounter during your visit:

International Film Selection: RIIFF features a curated selection of international films, including narrative features, documentaries, shorts, and animations. The festival provides a platform for filmmakers to share their unique stories and perspectives with a global audience.

Diverse Genres: The film lineup at RIIFF spans a wide range of genres, catering to various cinematic tastes. Whether you're a fan of drama, comedy, thriller, or experimental cinema, you're likely to find films that captivate and resonate with you.

Filmmaker Q&A Sessions: Many screenings are followed by Q&A sessions with filmmakers, directors, and cast members. These sessions provide insights into the creative process, the inspiration behind the films, and offer a chance for audience interaction.

Short Film Showcases: RIIFF often dedicates attention to short films, providing a platform for filmmakers to showcase their storytelling skills in a condensed format. Short film programs can be particularly diverse and showcase emerging talents.

Emerging Filmmakers: The festival is known for supporting emerging filmmakers and providing a launching pad for their careers. It's an opportunity to discover new voices in the world of cinema and witness fresh perspectives.

Industry Networking: RIIFF attracts not only film enthusiasts but also industry professionals. Attending the festival provides opportunities for networking, connecting with filmmakers, producers, and other individuals involved in the film industry.

Cinematic Diversity: The festival often emphasizes diversity and inclusion, showcasing films that represent different cultures, backgrounds, and experiences. This commitment to diversity contributes to a rich and inclusive cinematic experience.

Special Events and Gala Screenings: RIIFF may host special events, gala screenings, and awards ceremonies. These events add a touch of glamour to the festival and celebrate outstanding contributions to the world of cinema.

Educational Programs: In addition to film screenings, RIIFF may offer educational programs, workshops, and panel discussions. These initiatives provide valuable insights into various aspects of filmmaking and the film industry.

Exploration of Providence: While attending the festival, you have the opportunity to explore Providence, the host city. Discovering local attractions, dining at unique restaurants, and experiencing the cultural vibe of the city enhances your overall festival experience.

Cinematic Atmosphere: RIIFF creates a cinematic atmosphere throughout the host city, with film screenings held in various theaters and venues. The festival buzz extends beyond the screening rooms, creating an exciting and immersive environment for film enthusiasts.

Attending the Rhode Island International Film Festival is not just about watching films; it's about celebrating the art of storytelling, supporting emerging talents, and being part of a global cinematic community. The festival offers a dynamic and engaging experience for cinephiles and provides a platform for filmmakers to share their creative visions with a diverse and appreciative audience.

49. Take a day trip to Newport.

Embarking on a day trip to Newport promises a delightful blend of history, scenic beauty, and coastal charm. Here's a suggested itinerary for your day in Newport:

Morning:
Breakfast at a Local Cafe:
Start your day with a delicious breakfast at one of Newport's charming cafes. Consider places like Cru Cafe or Corner Café for a cozy and local experience.

Explore The Breakers:
Begin your exploration with a visit to The Breakers, a stunning Gilded Age mansion and a symbol of Newport's opulent history. Walk through the elaborate rooms and marvel at the architecture and ocean views.

Late Morning:
Cliff Walk:
Head to the Cliff Walk, a scenic path that winds along the shoreline, offering breathtaking views of the Atlantic Ocean and the backyards of Newport's

famous mansions. This picturesque walk combines natural beauty with architectural splendor.

Lunch:

Lunch on Thames Street:

Thames Street is a lively thoroughfare lined with shops and restaurants. Choose a restaurant like The Black Pearl or Brick Alley Pub for a delicious lunch with a view of the harbor.

Afternoon:

Visit the Newport Mansions:

Explore more of Newport's grand mansions. Depending on your interests, consider visiting Marble House, Rosecliff, or the historic Hunter House.

Stroll through Bowen's Wharf:

Wander around Bowen's Wharf, a historic waterfront area filled with shops, galleries, and eateries. It's a great place to pick up souvenirs or enjoy a sweet treat.

Mid-Afternoon:

Newport Art Museum:

If you have an interest in art, visit the Newport Art Museum. It features a diverse collection of American art and often hosts temporary exhibitions.

Relax at King Park:

Take a break at King Park, a waterfront park with lovely views of Newport Harbor. It's a peaceful spot to relax, have a picnic, or simply enjoy the maritime atmosphere.

Evening:

Dinner at Bannister's Wharf:

As the day winds down, head to Bannister's Wharf for dinner. The area offers a variety of dining options, from seafood restaurants like The Mooring to upscale choices like 22 Bowen's Wine Bar & Grille.

Newport Sunset Cruise:

End your day with a sunset cruise. Several companies offer evening cruises that provide stunning views of the sunset over Narragansett Bay.

Night:

Explore Thames Street at Night:

After the sun sets, take a stroll along Thames Street once again. The atmosphere changes, with shops illuminated and live music pouring out from pubs and cafes.

Nightcap at a Historic Pub:
Conclude your day trip with a nightcap at a historic pub like The White Horse Tavern, one of America's oldest taverns, dating back to 1673.

Additional Tips:
Check for any special events or festivals happening in Newport during your visit.
Wear comfortable shoes for walking, especially if you plan to explore the Cliff Walk.
Consider renting a bike to cover more ground and explore the city at a leisurely pace.
This itinerary offers a mix of history, outdoor beauty, and culinary delights, allowing you to make the most of your day trip to the charming coastal city of Newport.

50.Explore the Jewelry District Riverwalk.

Exploring the Jewelry District Riverwalk in Providence provides a scenic and tranquil experience along the waterfront. Here's a suggested itinerary for your exploration:

Morning:
Breakfast at a Local Cafe:
Start your day with a hearty breakfast at a local café. Consider establishments like Small Point Café or Bolt Coffee for a cozy and energizing start.

Begin at Davol Square:
Head to Davol Square, a historic area with red-brick buildings that once housed jewelry manufacturers. Take a moment to appreciate the architecture and the mix of old and new in this revitalized district.

Late Morning:
Riverwalk Stroll:
Begin your Riverwalk adventure. Follow the Riverwalk path along the Providence River. Enjoy the views of the water, passing boats, and the skyline of downtown Providence.

Point Street Bridge:

Walk across the Point Street Bridge for panoramic views of the river and the surrounding area. Capture some photos of the cityscape and the picturesque Waterplace Park.

Lunch:
Lunch at Hometown Poke:
As you continue your stroll, stop for lunch at Hometown Poke. This eatery offers a refreshing and customizable menu with poke bowls and other healthy options.

Afternoon:
Explore Waterplace Park:
Wander into Waterplace Park, known for its amphitheater and the popular WaterFire events. Enjoy the public art, sculptures, and the serene setting along the river.

Providence Pedestrian Bridge:
Walk along the Providence Pedestrian Bridge, a picturesque suspension bridge that connects the Jewelry District to the city's East Side. The views from the bridge are spectacular.

Mid-Afternoon:
Visit India Point Park:
Head to India Point Park, a waterfront park with walking trails and green spaces. It's an excellent spot to relax, have a picnic, or simply enjoy the riverside ambiance.

Coffee at Coffee Exchange:
If you need a pick-me-up, stop by Coffee Exchange, a local coffee shop known for its artisanal coffee blends. Take your coffee to go and continue exploring.

Evening:
Dinner at Plant City:
Conclude your day with dinner at Plant City, a unique vegan food hall with multiple dining options. Enjoy plant-based dishes in a stylish and eco-friendly setting.

Twilight Riverwalk:
Experience the Riverwalk during the twilight hours. The city lights reflecting on the water and the ambiance of the evening make for a magical atmosphere.

Night:

Nightlife at The Dorrance:
If you're in the mood for some nightlife, consider visiting The Dorrance, a historic restaurant and cocktail lounge. The elegant setting and crafted cocktails make it a great spot for an evening drink.
Additional Tips:
Check for any events or performances happening at Waterplace Park or nearby venues.
Wear comfortable shoes suitable for walking along the Riverwalk and bridges.
Take your time to appreciate the public art installations and sculptures along the route.
Exploring the Jewelry District Riverwalk offers a blend of natural beauty, urban charm, and culinary delights. Whether you're interested in a leisurely stroll, cultural exploration, or waterfront dining, this itinerary allows you to experience the best of this vibrant area in Providence.

51. Attend a WaterFire Basin Lighting event.

Attending a WaterFire Basin Lighting event in Providence is a captivating and immersive experience that combines art, culture, and community. Here's what you might encounter during your visit:

Evening:
Arrival at Waterplace Park:
Begin your evening by arriving at Waterplace Park, the central location for WaterFire events. The park is transformed with the setting sun, and the anticipation for the lighting ceremony builds.

Explore Waterplace Park:
Take some time to explore Waterplace Park before the lighting ceremony begins. Enjoy the scenic views, stroll along the riverwalk, and observe the preparations for the event.

Sunset:
Sunset Rituals:
WaterFire Basin Lighting events often coincide with sunset. Participate in any sunset rituals or performances that may be part of the program, setting the stage for the magical experience that follows.
Lighting Ceremony:
Ignition of the Fires:

As dusk falls, witness the mesmerizing ignition of the fires. The braziers set afloat on the water are lit one by one, creating a breathtaking display of light and reflection on the river.

Music and Performances:
Throughout the evening, enjoy live musical performances and artistic presentations. WaterFire events often feature a diverse range of musicians, performers, and artists who contribute to the enchanting atmosphere.

Nightfall:
Illuminated Waterways:
As night falls, the illuminated waterways come alive. The flickering flames on the water create a unique and magical ambiance, casting a warm glow on the surrounding architecture and landscape.

Bridge of Stars:
Walk along the "Bridge of Stars," where luminaria bags line the bridges, adding to the celestial atmosphere. This is a beautiful and symbolic element of the WaterFire experience.

Reflection and Contemplation:
Quiet Moments:
Find a quiet spot along the river to reflect and contemplate the beauty of the fires, the soothing sounds of the water, and the communal spirit of the event. WaterFire often encourages a sense of connection and contemplation.
Late Evening:
Riverside Dining:
Consider enjoying a late evening meal at one of the waterfront restaurants along the river. The combination of the fires and city lights creates a romantic and atmospheric backdrop.
Additional Tips:
Check the Schedule:
Be sure to check the WaterFire schedule for any additional events, performances, or special themes happening on the night you plan to attend.

Arrive Early:
To secure a good viewing spot and fully immerse yourself in the experience, consider arriving a bit earlier before the scheduled lighting time.

Dress Comfortably:

Wear comfortable clothing and footwear, especially if you plan to explore the area on foot.

Attending a WaterFire Basin Lighting event is not just about witnessing a spectacle; it's about participating in a communal celebration of art, light, and shared experiences. The combination of fire, water, and music creates a unique and memorable atmosphere that captures the essence of Providence's cultural richness.

52. Explore the Hope Street Farmers Market.

Exploring the Hope Street Farmers Market in Providence provides a vibrant and community-oriented experience. Here's a suggested itinerary for your visit:

Morning:
Arrival and Breakfast:
Start your day by arriving at the Hope Street Farmers Market, typically held on Saturdays. Many vendors offer breakfast options, so consider grabbing a fresh pastry or a hot beverage to kickstart your exploration.

Stroll Through the Market:
Begin your market adventure by strolling through the various vendor stalls. The market features local farmers, artisans, and food producers, offering a diverse array of products.

Late Morning:
Fresh Produce Shopping:
Explore the fresh produce section of the market. Purchase seasonal fruits, vegetables, and herbs directly from local farmers. This is an excellent opportunity to support local agriculture and enjoy the flavors of the region.

Artisanal Products:
Browse through stalls offering artisanal products. You might find handmade crafts, local honey, artisanal cheeses, baked goods, and other unique items that showcase the talents of local artisans.

Midday:
Live Music and Entertainment:
Enjoy the lively atmosphere with live music or entertainment that is often featured at the market. Local musicians and performers contribute to the festive and community-oriented vibe.

Lunch from Food Trucks:
If the market includes food trucks, consider trying a delicious lunch made from locally sourced ingredients. Whether it's a gourmet sandwich, a bowl of fresh salad, or a unique fusion dish, the food trucks add a culinary flair to the market experience.

Afternoon:
Community Engagement:
Engage with community organizations and local initiatives that might have informational booths at the market. Learn about sustainability efforts, community events, or how you can get involved in local projects.

Coffee and Desserts:
Take a break and indulge in a cup of freshly brewed coffee from a local vendor. Pair it with a delectable dessert, whether it's a pastry, cookie, or another sweet treat.

Late Afternoon:
Relax in Lippitt Park:
Lippitt Park, where the market is often held, provides a green and relaxing space. Take a seat, enjoy your purchases, and soak in the lively yet laid-back atmosphere.

Yoga or Fitness Classes:
Some markets offer fitness or yoga classes. Check the schedule to see if there are any wellness activities taking place during your visit. It's a great way to stay active while embracing the community spirit.

Additional Tips:
Reusable Bags:
Bring reusable bags to carry your purchases. Many farmers markets encourage sustainability, and using your own bags reduces waste.

Cash and Cards:
While many vendors accept cards, having some cash on hand is convenient, especially when dealing with smaller vendors or food trucks.

Check the Schedule:
The market may have special events, themed days, or guest vendors. Check the schedule in advance to make the most of your visit.

Travel to Providence Rhode Island

The Hope Street Farmers Market offers a delightful blend of fresh, local products, community engagement, and a lively atmosphere. Whether you're a local resident or a visitor, the market provides an authentic taste of Providence's local flavors and the opportunity to connect with the community.

53. Attend a drag show at The Dark Lady.

Attending a drag show at The Dark Lady in Providence promises a night of entertainment, creativity, and vibrant performances. Here's what you might experience during your visit:

Evening:
Arrival and Atmosphere:
Arrive at The Dark Lady, a well-known LGBTQ+ venue in Providence, and soak in the lively and welcoming atmosphere. The eclectic décor, dim lighting, and energetic vibe set the stage for an unforgettable evening.

Pre-Show Drinks:
Start your evening with pre-show drinks at the bar. The Dark Lady often offers a diverse selection of cocktails and beverages. Grab a seat, enjoy the music, and get into the celebratory mood.

Showtime:
Drag Performances:
As the show begins, prepare to be dazzled by the drag performers. Drag shows at The Dark Lady feature talented queens who showcase their artistry through lip-syncing, dance routines, and stunning outfits. Each performer brings a unique style and personality to the stage.

Audience Interaction:
Drag shows are known for their interactive nature. Don't be surprised if performers engage with the audience, bringing people on stage for playful moments or encouraging cheers and applause.

Mid-Show:
Variety of Performances:
Enjoy a variety of performances throughout the show. Drag queens may perform solo acts, group numbers, or even themed routines. The diversity of performances adds to the overall excitement.

Tips and Tipping Culture:
Tipping is a common practice at drag shows. Be prepared with some cash to tip the performers. It's a way to show appreciation for their talent and effort.

Late Evening:
Dance and Socialize:
After the drag show, The Dark Lady often transitions into a dance floor. Join the crowd on the dance floor and continue the celebration. The DJ typically plays a mix of upbeat music to keep the energy high.

Connect with Others:
The Dark Lady is a social hub, and drag shows provide an opportunity to connect with fellow attendees. Strike up conversations, make new friends, and share the joyous atmosphere.

Additional Tips:
Check the Schedule:
Before planning your visit, check The Dark Lady's schedule for drag show dates and any special events. Drag shows may have themed nights or guest performers.

Reservations:
Consider making reservations, especially if you're visiting on a popular night or during a special event. It ensures you have a spot and can fully enjoy the experience.

Dress Code:
Embrace the opportunity to dress up if you're inclined. While there may not be a strict dress code, many attendees choose to express themselves through creative and colorful attire.

Attending a drag show at The Dark Lady is not just about the performances; it's a celebration of self-expression, inclusivity, and the vibrant LGBTQ+ community. The combination of talent, music, and the energetic atmosphere makes for a memorable and uplifting night out in Providence.

54. Visit the John Brown Memorial Park.

Visiting the John Brown Memorial Park in Providence is a journey into the city's rich historical tapestry, specifically honoring the legacy of John Brown, a key figure in the 19th-century abolitionist movement. The park, nestled in a tranquil setting, serves as both a memorial and a reflection space, inviting visitors to delve into the profound impact of Brown's activism in the fight against slavery. The centerpiece of the park is a striking statue of John Brown, a poignant symbol of his unwavering commitment to the cause of liberation.

Surrounded by lush greenery and pathways, the park provides a serene environment conducive to contemplation. As you wander through the grounds, you'll notice informational plaques and markers that offer insights into John Brown's life, his contributions to the abolitionist movement, and the historical context in which he lived. The park's proximity to Brown University further underscores its significance, creating a nexus of history, education, and activism.

Beyond the statue, the park's design encourages a deeper connection to the broader narrative of Providence's role in the struggle for social justice. It serves as a reminder of the city's place in shaping the national discourse on human rights. The John Brown Memorial Park, with its thoughtfully landscaped spaces and peaceful ambiance, provides a unique opportunity for both locals and visitors to engage with history, fostering a greater understanding of the challenges faced and progress achieved in the pursuit of equality and justice. Whether one seeks a moment of quiet reflection or a more immersive exploration of Providence's historical roots, this park stands as a testament to the enduring relevance of John Brown's legacy in the ongoing journey towards a more just society.

55. Explore the East Side Marketplace.

Exploring the East Side Marketplace in Providence promises a delightful venture into a vibrant and community-focused shopping experience. Located on the city's East Side, this marketplace caters to a diverse array of tastes and preferences. Upon entering, you'll discover a lively atmosphere where local vendors and specialty shops converge to create a unique shopping destination.

The East Side Marketplace is renowned for its commitment to showcasing local and regional products. From fresh produce and artisanal goods to unique crafts and specialty foods, the marketplace reflects the rich tapestry of Providence's entrepreneurial spirit. Navigating the aisles, you'll encounter a bounty of fresh fruits, vegetables, and other culinary delights, often sourced directly from nearby farms.

What distinguishes the East Side Marketplace is its emphasis on community engagement. The friendly interactions with vendors and the personalized service contribute to a warm and welcoming atmosphere. It's not just a place to shop; it's an opportunity to connect with local producers, artisans, and fellow shoppers who share a passion for supporting the community.

The marketplace's layout is designed to facilitate a leisurely exploration, allowing visitors to discover hidden gems and uncover unique treasures. Whether you're in search of a distinctive gift, a gourmet treat, or a fresh bouquet of flowers, the East Side Marketplace offers a diverse range of options.

Beyond its role as a shopping hub, the marketplace often hosts events, tastings, and activities that foster a sense of community. It's not uncommon to find live music performances, cooking demonstrations, or seasonal celebrations that add an extra layer of enjoyment to the overall experience.

As you conclude your exploration, you'll likely leave with not only a bag full of carefully selected items but also a sense of connection to the local community. The East Side Marketplace stands as a testament to Providence's dedication to fostering local businesses, promoting sustainability, and creating a dynamic space where residents and visitors alike can partake in the joy of discovering and supporting the diverse offerings of this charming city.

56. Visit the Providence Magic Museum.

Visiting the Providence Magic Museum is a journey into the enchanting world of illusion and wonder, adding a touch of magic to your exploration of the city. Located in Providence, this museum is a haven for magic enthusiasts and curious minds alike. Upon entering, you'll find yourself immersed in a realm where the mysterious and the extraordinary come to life through the art of magic.

The museum showcases a diverse collection of magical artifacts, historical memorabilia, and interactive exhibits that provide insight into the fascinating history of magic. From vintage posters and props to rare books and iconic illusions, the exhibits offer a comprehensive look at the evolution of magic as an art form. The museum's commitment to preserving and celebrating the rich heritage of magic makes it a captivating destination for both novices and seasoned magic aficionados.

Travel to Providence Rhode Island

Throughout your visit, you may have the opportunity to witness live demonstrations and performances by skilled magicians, further enhancing the immersive experience. The interactive nature of the museum allows visitors to engage with the exhibits, gaining a deeper appreciation for the craftsmanship and ingenuity behind the illusions.

The Providence Magic Museum goes beyond being a mere collection of artifacts; it serves as an educational and entertaining space. Whether you're intrigued by the sleight of hand, mesmerized by optical illusions, or captivated by the stories behind famous magicians, the museum caters to a spectrum of magical interests.

Beyond its exhibits, the museum often hosts special events, workshops, and lectures, providing visitors with the chance to delve deeper into the secrets of the magical arts. It's a dynamic hub where the spirit of amazement and curiosity thrives, creating an atmosphere of magic that extends beyond the museum's walls.

As you leave the Providence Magic Museum, you'll likely carry with you a newfound appreciation for the artistry and mystery of magic. The museum stands as a testament to the enduring allure of illusion and the ability of magic to captivate and inspire awe, making it a must-visit destination for those seeking a magical escapade in the heart of Providence.

57.Attend a concert at Lupo's Heartbreak Hotel.

Attending a concert at Lupo's Heartbreak Hotel in Providence is an exhilarating and immersive experience that resonates with the city's vibrant music scene. Located in the historic downtown area, Lupo's has established itself as an iconic venue renowned for hosting a diverse array of musical performances. As you step into the venue, the eclectic atmosphere, characterized by its industrial-chic aesthetics and pulsating energy, sets the stage for an unforgettable night of live music.

The stage at Lupo's has witnessed performances by a myriad of artists, spanning various genres from rock and alternative to hip-hop and electronic. The venue's intimate setting allows for an up-close and personal connection between the performers and the audience, creating an electric ambiance that amplifies the impact of the live music experience.

The acoustics at Lupo's are designed to deliver a high-quality sound, ensuring that every note, beat, and lyric resonates with clarity and intensity. Whether you're a devoted fan of a specific artist or open to discovering new talent, the diverse lineup of concerts at Lupo's caters to a wide range of musical tastes.

The venue's history is intertwined with Providence's cultural fabric, having played host to legendary acts and emerging artists alike. It's not just a space for concerts; it's a cultural hub that contributes to the city's dynamic arts and entertainment landscape.

Throughout the concert, the dynamic crowd adds to the immersive experience, creating a collective energy that elevates the atmosphere. Lupo's Heartbreak Hotel is not merely a venue; it's a destination that fosters a sense of community among music enthusiasts who converge to celebrate the universal language of sound.

As you exit Lupo's after a night of music, you'll likely carry with you the echoes of an extraordinary performance and the memories of a shared musical journey with fellow fans. The venue's role in shaping Providence's identity as a city that pulsates with creativity and artistic expression makes attending a concert at Lupo's a cultural and sensory adventure that transcends the ordinary.

58. Take a scenic drive along Ocean Drive.

Embarking on a scenic drive along Ocean Drive in Newport promises a picturesque journey along the stunning coastline of Rhode Island. As you set out on this coastal route, you'll find yourself immersed in the natural beauty and historical charm that define Newport's scenic landscapes.

The drive along Ocean Drive offers captivating views of the Atlantic Ocean, with waves crashing against rugged cliffs and expansive vistas opening up before you. The salty sea breeze and the rhythmic sound of the ocean create a serene and invigorating atmosphere throughout the journey.

Historic mansions, each with its own architectural grandeur, line the route, showcasing the opulence of the Gilded Age. Notable landmarks like the Marble House, The Breakers, and the Rosecliff Mansion come into view, providing a glimpse into Newport's rich history and affluence.

Travel to Providence Rhode Island

The road winds through Fort Adams State Park, offering not only panoramic views but also the opportunity to explore the historic Fort Adams. The fort, with its military history and strategic location, adds a layer of cultural interest to the scenic drive.

Numerous pull-off points and overlooks along Ocean Drive invite you to pause and savor the coastal panoramas. Beavertail State Park, situated at the southern tip of Conanicut Island, provides a particularly breathtaking vantage point, allowing you to admire the convergence of Narragansett Bay and the Atlantic Ocean.

As you continue along the route, the changing hues of the ocean, the rocky shores, and the lush landscapes create a dynamic and ever-evolving visual spectacle. The route is particularly enchanting during sunrise or sunset, casting a warm glow over the coastal scenery.

The Ocean Drive experience is not just about the scenery; it's a journey through time, blending natural beauty with architectural splendor. The road, flanked by sea and sky, encourages a leisurely pace, inviting you to savor each moment and appreciate the coastal grandeur that defines Newport's Ocean Drive. Whether you're a local resident or a visitor, this scenic drive provides a rejuvenating escape and an opportunity to immerse yourself in the timeless allure of Rhode Island's coastal treasures.

59. Attend a performance at the Trinity Repertory Company.

Attending a performance at the Trinity Repertory Company in Providence promises an immersive and culturally enriching experience within the realm of live theater. Located in the heart of downtown Providence, the theater is renowned for its commitment to artistic excellence, diverse productions, and engaging storytelling.

As you enter the historic building that houses the Trinity Rep, you'll be welcomed by an atmosphere that exudes the rich legacy of theatrical arts. The company's dedication to providing thought-provoking and entertaining performances is reflected in the diverse range of plays, classic works, and contemporary productions that grace its stages.

The stages at Trinity Rep come to life with dynamic performances delivered by a talented ensemble of actors. The theater's intimate setting ensures that the audience is not just a passive observer but an active participant in the unfolding narrative. The nuanced acting, compelling set designs, and meticulous attention to detail contribute to a theatrical experience that transcends the ordinary.

Trinity Repertory Company's repertoire often includes a mix of classic plays, bold interpretations of Shakespearean works, and innovative contemporary productions. Whether you're a fan of timeless classics or eager to explore cutting-edge performances, the diverse programming at Trinity Rep caters to a wide range of theatrical preferences.

Beyond the main stage productions, Trinity Rep is committed to community engagement and educational outreach. The theater offers workshops, educational programs, and opportunities for aspiring actors, fostering a sense of inclusivity and accessibility to the world of theater.

Attending a performance at the Trinity Repertory Company is not just a night at the theater; it's an invitation to immerse yourself in the transformative power of storytelling. The communal experience of shared laughter, contemplation, and emotional resonance creates a unique bond among audience members, making the Trinity Rep an integral part of Providence's vibrant cultural landscape. Whether you're a seasoned theatergoer or a first-time attendee, the Trinity Repertory Company promises an unforgettable journey into the captivating world of live performance art.

60. Explore the Roger Williams Botanical Center.

Exploring the Roger Williams Park Botanical Center in Providence invites you into a lush and tranquil oasis where nature's beauty takes center stage. Nestled within Roger Williams Park, this botanical center is a haven for plant enthusiasts, nature lovers, and those seeking a serene escape within the city.

As you enter the botanical center, you'll discover a variety of themed indoor gardens, each meticulously curated to showcase diverse plant species from around the world. The Tropical Rainforest Conservatory, with its soaring palms and vibrant orchids, creates a microcosm of a tropical paradise. The Desert

Room, featuring succulents and cacti, transports visitors to arid landscapes, while the Mediterranean Room showcases flora from the Mediterranean region.

The center's educational displays and interpretive signage provide valuable insights into the ecological significance and cultural importance of various plant species. Visitors can embark on a self-guided tour, allowing for a leisurely exploration of the distinct botanical environments.

The outdoor gardens surrounding the center offer a breath of fresh air and an opportunity to experience the changing seasons. The themed gardens, including the Rose Maze and the Perennial Garden, boast an array of colors and fragrances, providing a picturesque backdrop for leisurely strolls and moments of quiet contemplation.

The Japanese Garden, designed with meticulous attention to detail, invites visitors to embrace the principles of tranquility and balance. Koi ponds, stone lanterns, and carefully pruned foliage contribute to the garden's serene ambiance.

Throughout the year, the Roger Williams Park Botanical Center hosts special events, workshops, and educational programs, further enriching the visitor experience. Whether you're interested in horticulture, sustainable gardening practices, or simply enjoying the beauty of blooming flowers, the center offers a diverse array of activities for all ages.

As you conclude your visit, you'll likely leave with a renewed appreciation for the botanical wonders that thrive within this urban sanctuary. The Roger Williams Park Botanical Center serves as a testament to the importance of biodiversity, environmental stewardship, and the joy that can be found in the diverse and interconnected world of plants.

61. Attend a WaterFire WaterFire for Recovery event.

Attending a WaterFire for Recovery event in Providence promises a poignant and uplifting experience that blends the transformative power of art with the spirit of community healing. WaterFire, renowned for its captivating fire-lit installations along the city's waterways, takes on a special significance during these events dedicated to recovery.

As you arrive at the WaterFire venue, you'll likely be greeted by the soft glow of the braziers reflecting on the water, creating a serene and contemplative atmosphere. The flickering flames, a signature element of WaterFire, symbolize hope, resilience, and the collective journey toward recovery.

The WaterFire for Recovery events often include unique elements and ceremonies that pay homage to individuals and communities overcoming challenges related to addiction, mental health, or other forms of recovery. The lighting of the fires becomes a symbolic act, representing the illumination of pathways to recovery and the shared commitment to supporting one another on this journey.

Live performances, including music, dance, and spoken word, may be integrated into the event, offering a platform for artistic expression and storytelling. These performances contribute to the emotional and cultural richness of the gathering, fostering connections and understanding among attendees.

Throughout the evening, you'll likely encounter various organizations and support networks providing resources, information, and assistance related to recovery and mental health. The collaborative effort of WaterFire and these organizations emphasizes the importance of community engagement and destigmatizing conversations around recovery.

The community-driven nature of WaterFire for Recovery events encourages a sense of inclusivity and empathy. Attendees, whether directly impacted by recovery or there in support, participate in a shared experience that transcends individual struggles and fosters a sense of unity.

As you witness the fires dancing on the water, reflecting the collective strength and resilience of those on the path to recovery, you'll likely be moved by the power of community, compassion, and the transformative impact of art in fostering healing and understanding. Attending a WaterFire for Recovery event is not just an observation of art but a participatory and reflective experience that contributes to the broader narrative of hope and recovery in the Providence community.

62. Take a hike in Lincoln Woods State Park.

Embarking on a hike in Lincoln Woods State Park offers a refreshing escape into nature, providing a diverse and picturesque landscape for outdoor

Travel to Providence Rhode Island

enthusiasts. Located in Lincoln, Rhode Island, this state park encompasses over 600 acres, offering an array of trails, woodlands, and water features.

As you begin your hike, you'll find a network of well-maintained trails that wind through dense forests, open meadows, and alongside serene ponds. The park's varied terrain caters to hikers of all skill levels, from casual strollers to more experienced trekkers seeking a challenge.

One popular trail is the Around-the-Pond Trail, which encircles Olney Pond, providing stunning water views and opportunities for birdwatching. The path is relatively flat, making it accessible for all ages, and features scenic spots for picnics or simply enjoying the tranquil surroundings.

For those seeking a more vigorous hike, the park offers interconnected trails like the Ridge Trail and the Quinsnicket Trail, which lead to elevated vantage points offering panoramic views of the surrounding landscape. The trails meander through rocky terrain and wooded areas, creating a sense of adventure and exploration.

Throughout your hike, you may encounter diverse flora and fauna, adding to the park's ecological richness. Keep an eye out for the vibrant colors of wildflowers, the rustle of leaves as you walk through wooded sections, and the possibility of spotting wildlife like birds, squirrels, and turtles.

Lincoln Woods State Park also provides opportunities for other outdoor activities, such as fishing, kayaking, and rock climbing. The Boulderwood section of the park features massive glacial boulders, attracting rock climbers looking for a unique challenge.

Whether you choose a leisurely stroll or a more challenging hike, Lincoln Woods State Park offers a serene and immersive natural experience, making it an ideal destination for a day of outdoor exploration. As you navigate the trails, you'll likely appreciate the park's ability to provide a peaceful retreat just a short distance from the hustle and bustle of urban life, creating a haven for both relaxation and adventure.

63. Visit the Roger Williams Park Carousel Village.

Visiting the Roger Williams Park Carousel Village in Providence promises a charming and nostalgic experience in a picturesque setting. Nestled within Roger Williams Park, this attraction combines the timeless joy of a carousel ride with a village-like atmosphere, creating a delightful destination for families and visitors of all ages.

As you approach the Carousel Village, the sight of a beautifully restored carousel immediately captures your attention. The carousel, adorned with intricately painted horses and other whimsical figures, stands as a classic centerpiece that evokes a sense of childhood wonder. The inviting music and the gentle rotation of the carousel create an enchanting ambiance.

The village setting around the carousel adds to the overall charm. You'll find a collection of quaint shops, food vendors, and recreational areas that contribute to the festive atmosphere. The village often hosts seasonal events, making it a dynamic and lively space throughout the year.

For families, the Carousel Village offers more than just carousel rides. The Hasbro Boundless Playground, located nearby, provides a space for children to explore and play. The playground is designed to be inclusive, featuring accessible equipment for children of all abilities.

The nearby Roger Williams Park Zoo and the Botanical Center offer additional opportunities for exploration, making the Carousel Village a central hub within the larger Roger Williams Park. Visitors can easily extend their outing to include a visit to these neighboring attractions, creating a well-rounded and enjoyable day in the park.

During special occasions or holidays, the Carousel Village often hosts themed events, adding an extra layer of excitement. Whether it's a summer carnival, a fall festival, or a winter holiday celebration, the village becomes a hub of activity, drawing locals and tourists alike.

As you leave the Carousel Village, you'll likely carry with you the nostalgic echoes of carousel music and the joyful laughter of visitors. The Roger Williams Park Carousel Village stands as a testament to the enduring appeal of simple pleasures and community spaces that bring people together for shared moments of happiness and connection.

64. Explore the Thayer Street shopping district.

Exploring the Thayer Street shopping district in Providence offers a vibrant and eclectic experience, characterized by a diverse array of shops, boutiques, eateries, and a lively atmosphere. Located near Brown University and the Rhode Island School of Design (RISD), Thayer Street is a popular destination for both locals and visitors seeking a mix of trendy fashion, unique finds, and delicious dining options.

As you wander along Thayer Street, you'll encounter a blend of independently-owned boutiques and well-known brands, creating a dynamic shopping environment. Fashion enthusiasts can explore clothing stores offering a range of styles, from bohemian chic to urban streetwear. Specialty shops showcase handmade jewelry, accessories, and art, reflecting the artistic and creative energy of the nearby universities.

Bookstores and art supply shops cater to the academic community, offering a selection of literature, textbooks, and art materials. The district's proximity to Brown University and RISD contributes to a culturally rich environment, influencing the unique character of the shops and the overall ambiance.

Thayer Street is not just a haven for fashion and art; it's also a culinary destination. The street is lined with diverse restaurants, cafes, and eateries serving a variety of cuisines. From cozy coffee shops to international flavors, the dining options cater to a wide range of tastes and preferences.

The street's lively atmosphere is heightened by street performers, local events, and a sense of community. During weekends and special occasions, Thayer Street often hosts festivals, markets, or live music, creating a festive and engaging environment for shoppers and strollers alike.

Beyond shopping and dining, Thayer Street is home to cultural landmarks like the Avon Cinema, an independent movie theater showcasing a mix of mainstream and indie films. The street's dynamic energy extends into the evening, with cafes and bars offering a social hub for locals and students.

Whether you're in search of unique fashion, artistic creations, or a diverse culinary experience, exploring the Thayer Street shopping district provides an immersive journey into the cultural and creative heartbeat of Providence. The district's blend of academic influence, independent spirit, and community vibrancy makes it a compelling destination for those seeking a memorable and multifaceted urban experience.

65. Attend a WaterFire Clear Currents event.

Attending a WaterFire Clear Currents event in Providence is a unique and captivating experience that combines the mesmerizing allure of WaterFire with a focus on environmental awareness and sustainability. Clear Currents events, held periodically, elevate the traditional WaterFire installation to incorporate themes centered around water, conservation, and the interconnectedness of communities.

As you arrive at the venue, you'll likely be greeted by the iconic sight of flickering bonfires on the water, casting a warm and reflective glow. The fires, carefully arranged in the river, serve as both an artistic spectacle and a symbolic representation of the elemental theme—water.

Clear Currents events often incorporate visual art installations, performances, and educational displays that highlight the importance of preserving water resources and fostering a sense of responsibility towards the environment. Local artists may contribute works that reflect the theme, creating an immersive and thought-provoking atmosphere along the riverbanks.

Educational initiatives and interactive exhibits may be set up to engage attendees in conversations about water conservation, sustainability practices, and the impact of human activities on aquatic ecosystems. The event becomes a platform for raising awareness and fostering a sense of environmental stewardship within the community.

Live performances, including music, dance, and theatrical presentations, may be curated to complement the event's theme. These performances often carry messages of interconnectedness, resilience, and the need for collective action in safeguarding water resources.

Clear Currents events are designed to be inclusive and family-friendly, offering a multi-sensory experience that appeals to a diverse audience. The combination of artistic expression, community engagement, and environmental advocacy creates a unique and impactful event that extends beyond the traditional WaterFire experience.

As you participate in a WaterFire Clear Currents event, you'll likely leave not only with the visual and auditory memories of a spectacular fire installation but also with a heightened awareness of the crucial role water plays in our lives and the shared responsibility we bear in preserving this vital resource. Attending such an event becomes a celebration of art, nature, and the collective commitment to a sustainable and vibrant future for the community and the planet.

66. Visit the Governor Sprague Mansion Museum.

Visiting the Governor Sprague Mansion Museum in Cranston, Rhode Island, provides a fascinating journey into the state's history, offering a glimpse into the lives of its prominent residents and the cultural heritage of the region. The mansion, a historic landmark, is a well-preserved example of 19th-century architecture and serves as a testament to Rhode Island's rich past.

Upon arriving at the mansion, you'll likely be struck by its imposing exterior, showcasing the architectural styles prevalent during the mid-1800s. Originally built in 1790 and later expanded and renovated by the Sprague family in the 1860s, the mansion exudes a sense of grandeur and historical significance.

Guided tours of the Governor Sprague Mansion provide an immersive experience, taking visitors through the various rooms and highlighting the mansion's architectural features, period furnishings, and the personal stories of the Sprague family. The mansion was home to several generations of the Sprague family, including two Rhode Island governors, and played a role in the state's political and industrial history.

As you explore the mansion, you'll encounter elegantly furnished rooms, ornate woodwork, and artifacts that offer a window into the lifestyle of the affluent during the 19th century. The museum often hosts exhibits and displays that delve into the cultural and social context of the mansion's era, providing a more comprehensive understanding of its historical significance.

The grounds surrounding the mansion add to the overall charm, with well-maintained gardens and pathways that invite visitors to take a leisurely stroll.

The mansion's location within the historical Pawtuxet Village enhances the experience, allowing visitors to further explore the surrounding area and appreciate its colonial charm.

The Governor Sprague Mansion Museum is not just a static repository of artifacts; it's a living testament to the stories and legacies of the people who shaped Rhode Island's history. Whether you're a history enthusiast, a lover of architecture, or simply curious about the past, a visit to the Governor Sprague Mansion Museum offers a captivating journey back in time, fostering a deeper appreciation for the cultural heritage of Cranston and the broader Rhode Island community.

67. Explore the Ten Mile River Greenway.

Exploring the Ten Mile River Greenway in Rhode Island offers a scenic and tranquil outdoor experience, allowing visitors to immerse themselves in nature while enjoying a network of trails and waterways. This greenway, stretching along the Ten Mile River, provides a peaceful escape in the midst of urban surroundings.

As you embark on the greenway, you'll likely encounter a well-maintained trail system that meanders alongside the river, offering a mix of paved paths and natural surfaces. The trail is suitable for various activities, including walking, jogging, biking, and birdwatching. The flat terrain makes it accessible to people of all fitness levels, creating a welcoming environment for both casual strolls and more active pursuits.

The lush greenery along the Ten Mile River adds to the scenic beauty, creating a serene backdrop for outdoor enthusiasts. The river itself contributes to the overall ambiance, with its gentle flow and the soothing sounds of water providing a calming effect. Depending on the season, you may witness vibrant foliage in the fall, blossoming flowers in the spring, and a serene winter landscape.

The greenway often features rest areas, benches, and interpretive signage that provide information about the local ecosystem, wildlife, and the history of the area. These amenities enhance the overall experience, offering opportunities for relaxation and learning as you traverse the trail.

Travel to Providence Rhode Island

Bridges and crossings along the greenway connect different sections, allowing for a continuous and varied journey. The network of trails may lead to adjacent parks, recreational areas, or community spaces, providing additional opportunities for exploration.

The Ten Mile River Greenway is not only a natural oasis but also a haven for birdwatchers and wildlife enthusiasts. Keep an eye out for diverse bird species and other local fauna that inhabit the riverbanks and surrounding vegetation.

Whether you're seeking a peaceful retreat for contemplation or a revitalizing outdoor adventure, the Ten Mile River Greenway provides a versatile and accessible escape. The greenway's role in promoting a connection to nature, fostering a sense of well-being, and offering recreational opportunities makes it a valuable asset for the local community and a destination worth exploring for anyone seeking a refreshing outdoor experience in Rhode Island.

68. Attend a show at the Providence Improv Guild.

Attending a show at the Providence Improv Guild (PIG) promises a night filled with laughter, spontaneity, and the infectious energy of live improvisational comedy. Located in the heart of Providence, PIG has established itself as a hub for local and emerging improv talent, offering a dynamic and engaging experience for audiences.

As you enter the intimate and laid-back atmosphere of the Providence Improv Guild, you'll likely sense the anticipation and excitement in the air. The venue's commitment to fostering a welcoming and inclusive environment sets the stage for a memorable night of unscripted comedy.

Improv shows at PIG are characterized by quick-witted performers who create scenes, characters, and narratives on the spot, often inspired by audience suggestions. The unpredictability of improv adds an element of surprise, ensuring that no two shows are ever the same. The performers' ability to think on their feet, collaborate seamlessly, and elicit genuine laughter from the audience contributes to the charm of the experience.

The Providence Improv Guild often hosts a variety of shows, including short-form improv games, long-form improv narratives, and themed performances.

The diversity of formats ensures that there's something for everyone, whether you're a seasoned improv enthusiast or a first-time attendee.

Audience participation is a key element of improv, and you might find yourself engaged in interactive moments that add to the fun. The connection between performers and audience members creates a shared experience, fostering a sense of camaraderie in the laughter-filled space.

Beyond regular shows, PIG may offer improv workshops and classes, providing opportunities for individuals to explore their own comedic talents and learn the fundamentals of improvisation.

Leaving a show at the Providence Improv Guild, you'll likely carry with you the echoes of laughter, the spontaneity of the performances, and a sense of joy that comes from witnessing the creativity of improv comedy. The Providence Improv Guild stands as a testament to the thriving arts and entertainment scene in Providence, offering a lighthearted and entertaining escape for those in search of laughter and a good time.

69. Take a walk through Swan Point Cemetery.

Taking a walk through Swan Point Cemetery in Providence provides a serene and contemplative experience within a historic and beautifully landscaped setting. Swan Point Cemetery, established in 1846, is not only a final resting place but also a picturesque green space, reflecting the Victorian-era concept of rural or garden cemeteries.

As you enter Swan Point, you'll likely be struck by the peaceful atmosphere and the meticulous design of the landscape. The cemetery is known for its scenic beauty, featuring rolling hills, mature trees, and well-maintained paths that wind through the grounds. The layout of the cemetery encourages a leisurely stroll, allowing visitors to appreciate the natural beauty and architectural elements.

Swan Point Cemetery is the final resting place for many notable individuals, including politicians, business leaders, and cultural figures. The cemetery's historical significance is evident in the diverse range of monuments, mausoleums, and grave markers that reflect the artistic and architectural styles of different eras.

The cemetery is also home to Swan Point Chapel, an architectural gem designed by the renowned architect H. H. Richardson. The chapel, with its Romanesque Revival style, adds a spiritual and cultural dimension to the landscape.

During your walk, you may encounter wildlife, including various bird species, adding to the sense of tranquility. Many visitors appreciate the seasonal changes, with spring blooms, summer greenery, and autumn foliage enhancing the visual appeal of the cemetery.

Swan Point Cemetery provides a reflective space for those seeking a connection with history, nature, or a quiet retreat from the bustle of urban life. The well-maintained grounds, the historical significance of the site, and the thoughtful design make it a place for both contemplation and appreciation of the interconnectedness of life and death.

Whether you're interested in history, architecture, or simply seeking a peaceful outdoor stroll, taking a walk through Swan Point Cemetery offers a unique and contemplative experience. It's a reminder that cemeteries can be not only places of remembrance but also vibrant landscapes that contribute to the cultural and natural tapestry of a community.

70.Explore the West Side Marketplace.

Exploring the West Side Marketplace in Providence offers a dynamic and diverse urban experience, combining shopping, dining, and cultural elements within a vibrant community setting. Located on the city's West Side, this marketplace reflects the eclectic and inclusive character of the neighborhood, providing an immersive journey into the local scene.

As you navigate the West Side Marketplace, you'll likely encounter a mix of independently-owned shops, boutiques, and eateries that contribute to the area's unique charm. The marketplace is known for its commitment to supporting local businesses, fostering a sense of community, and showcasing the creativity of Providence's entrepreneurs.

Boutiques and specialty stores offer an array of goods, ranging from handmade crafts and unique gifts to vintage finds and contemporary fashion. The marketplace is a haven for those seeking one-of-a-kind items and a departure from mainstream retail experiences.

The culinary scene at the West Side Marketplace is equally diverse. Local cafes, bakeries, and restaurants serve up a variety of cuisines, reflecting the multicultural fabric of the community. From cozy coffee shops to international eateries, the dining options cater to a broad range of tastes and preferences.

The marketplace often hosts events, festivals, and markets that bring the community together. These gatherings may feature live music, art displays, and opportunities to engage with local artists and artisans. Such events contribute to the festive atmosphere of the marketplace and provide additional layers of cultural richness.

The West Side Marketplace is not just a commercial hub; it's also a place for socializing and connecting with the neighborhood. Sidewalk seating, public spaces, and community events create a welcoming environment for residents and visitors alike. The sense of community engagement and the marketplace's role as a cultural focal point make it a destination where people come together to celebrate the local spirit.

Exploring the West Side Marketplace is not just about shopping and dining; it's a chance to immerse yourself in the creative energy of a neighborhood, support local businesses, and experience the diverse and inclusive essence of Providence's West Side. Whether you're a seasoned local or a first-time visitor, the marketplace invites you to discover the authenticity and vibrancy that define this dynamic urban space.

71. Attend a Providence Roller Derby match.

Attending a Providence Roller Derby match promises an exhilarating and action-packed experience that combines athleticism, skill, and the vibrant spirit of roller derby culture. Providence Roller Derby, a dynamic and competitive league, showcases the strength, strategy, and camaraderie inherent in this fast-paced sport.

As you enter the venue, you'll likely be greeted by the energetic atmosphere of roller derby enthusiasts and fans. The sound of wheels on the track, the cheers from the crowd, and the anticipation of the match create a unique and lively ambiance.

Roller derby matches typically consist of two teams of roller skaters competing against each other on an oval track. Each team has a jammer, whose goal is to score points by lapping members of the opposing team, while blockers and pivots work together to impede the progress of the opposing jammer and assist their own jammer.

The physicality and strategy involved in roller derby make for an engaging spectator experience. The athletes' agility, speed, and strategic maneuvers, coupled with the occasional collisions and dramatic moments, contribute to the excitement of the match. The bouts are not only about athletic prowess but also about teamwork, communication, and adaptability on the track.

Providence Roller Derby events often include halftime entertainment, merchandise booths, and opportunities to meet the skaters, adding to the overall fan experience. The league may also host themed events, fundraisers, and after-parties, fostering a sense of community among fans and participants.

Whether you're a roller derby enthusiast or a newcomer to the sport, attending a Providence Roller Derby match is an opportunity to witness the dynamic and empowering world of roller derby. The dedication, athleticism, and team spirit displayed by the skaters create an entertaining and inspiring experience that resonates with the inclusive and empowering ethos of roller derby culture.

72. Attend the Federal Hill Summer Festival.

Attending the Federal Hill Summer Festival in Providence promises a lively and festive experience celebrating the vibrant culture, cuisine, and community spirit of the Federal Hill neighborhood. Federal Hill is renowned for its Italian heritage, and the Summer Festival often highlights the rich traditions, delicious food, and lively atmosphere that make this area a cultural hub.

As you arrive at the festival, you'll likely be immersed in a kaleidoscope of sights and sounds. The streets come alive with vibrant decorations, street vendors, and the enticing aroma of Italian and international cuisine wafting through the air. The Summer Festival typically showcases the diverse culinary offerings of Federal Hill, with local restaurants and food vendors serving up a variety of delicious dishes.

Live music, entertainment, and cultural performances contribute to the festive atmosphere, providing a backdrop of celebration for attendees. Whether it's traditional Italian folk music, contemporary performances, or dance displays, the entertainment lineup is designed to appeal to a broad audience and create an engaging experience.

The festival often features activities for all ages, including games, arts and crafts, and family-friendly entertainment. Local businesses and artisans may set up booths, offering a range of products and unique finds for festival-goers to explore.

The Federal Hill Summer Festival is not only a celebration of food and entertainment but also an opportunity to experience the tight-knit community spirit of this historic neighborhood. It's a chance for residents and visitors alike to come together, share in the joy of summer, and appreciate the cultural diversity that defines Federal Hill.

Keep in mind that specific details about the Federal Hill Summer Festival, including dates, performers, and activities, may vary from year to year. For the most up-to-date information on the festival schedule and offerings, I recommend checking with local event organizers or the official Providence tourism office.

73. Take a historical walking tour of Providence.

Embarking on a historical walking tour of Providence offers a captivating journey through the city's rich past, showcasing its architectural gems, cultural landmarks, and key historical sites. As you explore the streets of Providence, you'll encounter a blend of colonial, Federal, Victorian, and modern structures that collectively tell the story of the city's evolution over the centuries.

Begin your walking tour in the College Hill neighborhood, known for its historic charm and significant landmarks. Visit the John Brown House Museum, an 18th-century mansion that provides insight into the life of one of Providence's prominent families during the colonial era.

Continue to Benefit Street, often referred to as the "Mile of History." This enchanting street is lined with well-preserved historic homes, including the Governor Stephen Hopkins House and the Old State House, which served as the state capitol building from 1762 to 1904.

Travel to Providence Rhode Island

As you stroll through Waterplace Park, you'll encounter the iconic WaterFire installation, an art installation featuring bonfires on the river, transforming the area into a magical display. Learn about the city's industrial history at the Providence Athenaeum, a historic library dating back to 1836.

Explore the campuses of Brown University and the Rhode Island School of Design (RISD), both integral to Providence's cultural and intellectual identity. The RISD Museum is a noteworthy stop, housing a diverse collection of art spanning different periods and cultures.

Take a moment to appreciate the beauty of Prospect Terrace Park, which offers panoramic views of downtown Providence and features a statue of H.P. Lovecraft, the renowned American writer.

Visit the Roger Williams National Memorial, dedicated to the city's founder, Roger Williams, and gain insights into the principles of religious freedom that shaped Providence's early history.

In the Jewelry District, discover the historic buildings that once housed jewelry manufacturers and explore the nearby Fox Point neighborhood, known for its maritime history.

Your walking tour can also include stops at the Rhode Island State House, the Providence Performing Arts Center, and other landmarks that contribute to the city's diverse tapestry of history and culture. Consider joining a guided walking tour to enhance your experience with expert insights and historical anecdotes.

74. Attend a WaterFire Salute to Veterans event.

Attending a WaterFire Salute to Veterans event in Providence is a poignant and patriotic experience that honors and celebrates the service of veterans. WaterFire, known for its enchanting bonfire installations on the rivers of downtown Providence, transforms into a special tribute during these events, creating a moving and symbolic atmosphere.

As you arrive at the venue, you'll likely be greeted by the glow of the bonfires reflecting on the water, creating a serene and contemplative setting. The Salute to Veterans events often feature unique and solemn elements that pay tribute to the men and women who have served in the armed forces.

The lighting of the bonfires is accompanied by musical performances, ceremonies, and presentations that highlight the sacrifices and contributions of veterans. The music, often chosen to evoke a sense of reverence and gratitude, adds a powerful emotional layer to the experience.

Throughout the event, you may encounter military displays, exhibits, and interactive activities that provide opportunities for attendees to learn more about the history of veterans' service and the importance of honoring their commitment to the nation.

The presence of veterans, active-duty military personnel, and their families contributes to the sense of community and shared appreciation. The events are often designed to be inclusive, inviting the public to join in expressing gratitude and support for those who have served.

The WaterFire Salute to Veterans events may also include moments of reflection, such as a ring of the bells, a moment of silence, or other rituals that add to the solemnity of the occasion. These elements serve to create a space for remembrance, appreciation, and unity within the community.

Attending a WaterFire Salute to Veterans event is not only an opportunity to witness the magical spectacle of WaterFire but also a chance to participate in a meaningful and collective expression of gratitude for the service and sacrifice of veterans. The events serve as a reminder of the enduring connection between the arts, community, and the recognition of those who have dedicated their lives to the defense of freedom.

75. Explore the Providence Arcade, the oldest shopping mall in the U.S.

Exploring the Providence Arcade is a journey back in time, as it holds the distinction of being the oldest shopping mall in the United States. Located in the heart of downtown Providence, the arcade is a historic landmark that offers a unique blend of architectural charm, boutique shops, and a touch of nostalgia.

Constructed in 1828, the Providence Arcade is an early example of Greek Revival architecture. Its iconic white columns and grand facade contribute to the visual appeal and historical significance of the building. The arcade was designed by architects Russell Warren and James Bucklin, and its purpose was to provide a covered shopping space for local merchants and customers.

As you enter the arcade, you'll be greeted by a charming interior that preserves the ambiance of a bygone era. The building features a glass roof that allows natural light to filter through, creating a bright and airy atmosphere. The two levels of the arcade are lined with small shops and boutiques, offering a range of products from unique gifts and handmade crafts to clothing and accessories.

The Providence Arcade underwent a significant renovation in recent years to preserve its historical integrity while adapting to contemporary needs. The restoration effort aimed to maintain the original architectural elements while creating a modern and vibrant space for businesses and visitors.

Walking through the arcade, you'll likely encounter a mix of local businesses, cafes, and specialty shops. The arcade has become a hub for independent retailers and artisans, contributing to its role as a cultural and commercial center within the city.

The Providence Arcade is not just a shopping destination; it's a piece of living history that has evolved with the times. Whether you're interested in exploring its architectural significance, supporting local businesses, or simply enjoying a leisurely stroll through a historic space, the arcade offers a distinctive and charming experience that reflects the enduring character of Providence.

76. Take a day trip to Block Island.

Embarking on a day trip to Block Island from Providence offers a scenic and relaxing getaway, allowing you to explore the island's natural beauty, charming beaches, and unique attractions. Here's a suggested itinerary for your day trip:

Morning: Departure and Arrival

Ferry Ride: Begin your day trip by taking a ferry from Point Judith or another nearby ferry terminal to Block Island. Enjoy the scenic views during the ferry ride, and keep an eye out for any marine life that might make an appearance.

Arrival at Old Harbor: Once you arrive at Old Harbor on Block Island, take some time to explore the quaint town. You'll find shops, cafes, and bike rental places around the harbor.

Late Morning: Explore the Town
3. Block Island Historical Society: Visit the Block Island Historical Society to learn about the island's history. The society often has exhibits showcasing the island's maritime heritage, lighthouses, and more.

Settlers' Rock: Take a stroll to Settlers' Rock, a historical marker commemorating the island's early settlers. It's a peaceful spot with beautiful views.
Lunch: Dining with a View
5. The Oar Restaurant: Head to The Oar Restaurant for lunch. This waterfront eatery is known for its delicious seafood and has outdoor seating with scenic views of the harbor.

Afternoon: Nature and Relaxation
6. Mohegan Bluffs: Spend the afternoon exploring Mohegan Bluffs. These majestic clay cliffs offer breathtaking views of the Atlantic Ocean. You can descend the stairs to the beach below if you're up for a little adventure.

Southeast Lighthouse: Visit the Southeast Lighthouse, a historic structure with panoramic views. The adjacent Mohegan Bluffs provide a stunning backdrop.
Late Afternoon: Beach Time
8. Ballard's Beach: Relax and unwind at Ballard's Beach. It's a popular spot with a beachfront bar where you can enjoy a refreshing drink while taking in the ocean breeze.

Evening: Sunset and Departure
9. North Light: Head to North Light to catch the sunset. This iconic lighthouse offers a picturesque setting as the sun dips below the horizon.

Dinner in Old Harbor: Before catching the ferry back to the mainland, have dinner in Old Harbor. There are several restaurants offering diverse cuisines to suit your preferences.
Night: Ferry Ride Back
11. Ferry Ride Back: Board the ferry for your return trip, enjoying the evening views of the water and the mainland in the distance.

This itinerary provides a mix of historical exploration, natural beauty, and relaxation on Block Island, making the most of your day trip from Providence.

Travel to Providence Rhode Island

77. Attend a WaterFire FireBall event.

Attending a WaterFire FireBall event in Providence is an extraordinary and unforgettable experience that goes beyond the ordinary gala affair. This annual event, organized by WaterFire Providence, transcends traditional fundraising gatherings, bringing together an eclectic mix of art, music, and community spirit against the enchanting backdrop of the city's waterways. The FireBall is a celebration of creativity and philanthropy, and attendees can expect an evening filled with sophistication and allure.

As the night unfolds, guests are welcomed into a world of visual splendor and artistic expression. The iconic WaterFire installations, with their flickering flames reflected on the water's surface, set the stage for an ambiance that is both mesmerizing and magical. The event often features captivating live performances, further enhancing the sensory experience and adding an extra layer of cultural richness to the night.

The culinary offerings at the FireBall are nothing short of exquisite, showcasing the talents of local chefs and caterers. Attendees can indulge in a culinary journey that complements the artistic atmosphere, with a diverse array of gourmet delights and beverages served throughout the evening. The attention to detail in both the culinary and artistic aspects of the event creates a seamless and immersive experience for all.

Beyond the aesthetic pleasures, the FireBall serves a noble cause. It stands as a testament to the community's support for WaterFire Providence, an organization dedicated to promoting the arts and fostering a sense of unity in the city. Funds raised during the event contribute to the continued success of WaterFire's impactful and transformative projects, ensuring that the magic of WaterFire can continue to captivate residents and visitors alike.

In essence, attending a WaterFire FireBall event is not just about an evening of glamour and entertainment; it's a celebration of the arts, a demonstration of community solidarity, and a chance to contribute to the cultural vibrancy that defines Providence. Each year, the FireBall weaves a narrative of creativity, philanthropy, and celebration, making it an unmissable highlight in the city's social calendar.

78. Explore the Roger Williams National Memorial Visitor Center.

Exploring the Roger Williams National Memorial Visitor Center in Providence offers a fascinating journey into the history of religious freedom and the life of Roger Williams, the founder of Rhode Island and a key figure in the early development of the United States. Housed within the visitor center are exhibits, artifacts, and informative displays that provide a comprehensive understanding of Williams' contributions and the principles he championed.

Upon entering the visitor center, you'll likely encounter exhibits that delve into the life and legacy of Roger Williams. Through interactive displays, historical documents, and multimedia presentations, visitors can gain insights into Williams' advocacy for the separation of church and state, his interactions with Native American communities, and the establishment of the colony of Rhode Island as a haven for religious freedom.

Artifacts from the 17th century, including documents, tools, and personal items associated with Roger Williams, may be on display, providing a tangible connection to the historical context. The visitor center's design is often thoughtfully curated to enhance the learning experience, with visual elements that transport visitors back to the time of Roger Williams.

Knowledgeable park rangers or guides are typically available to offer additional information, answer questions, and provide context to the exhibits. Their insights help visitors appreciate the significance of Roger Williams' ideas in shaping the principles of religious liberty and tolerance in the early days of American history.

The Roger Williams National Memorial Visitor Center serves as an educational resource, aiming to inspire reflection on the importance of religious freedom and the enduring values that continue to shape the nation. Whether you are a history enthusiast or a casual visitor, exploring the center offers a meaningful and thought-provoking experience that contributes to a deeper understanding of the roots of American ideals.

79. Take a Providence Segway Tour.

Embarking on a Providence Segway Tour provides a unique and entertaining way to explore the city's highlights, historical sites, and scenic landscapes. Riding a Segway allows you to cover more ground than a walking tour while still enjoying the flexibility to stop and appreciate points of interest along the way.

As you begin your Segway adventure, you'll likely receive a brief orientation and training session to ensure you feel comfortable and confident maneuvering the Segway. Once you're acquainted with the controls, your tour guide will lead you through Providence's charming streets, sharing historical anecdotes and interesting facts about the city's landmarks.

The tour may take you to iconic sites such as Benefit Street, known for its colonial architecture and historic homes. Glide along the riverfront, enjoying picturesque views of Waterplace Park and the Providence skyline. Explore College Hill and its renowned institutions like Brown University and the Rhode Island School of Design (RISD), immersing yourself in the vibrant energy of these academic and cultural hubs.

Cruise through downtown Providence, passing by landmarks like the State House, the Providence Performing Arts Center, and the bustling Federal Hill neighborhood. The Segway's agility allows you to effortlessly navigate both historic districts and modern urban spaces, providing a comprehensive overview of the city's diverse character.

A Segway tour in Providence often includes stops at key points of interest, allowing you to take in the surroundings, capture photos, and absorb the rich history and culture of the city. The tour guides, often locals with in-depth knowledge, may share anecdotes and stories that bring the city to life, offering a personalized and engaging experience.

Whether you're a first-time visitor or a seasoned local, a Providence Segway Tour provides a fun and efficient way to explore the city's landmarks, neighborhoods, and scenic spots. It offers a fresh perspective on Providence's history and culture, making for an enjoyable and memorable experience on two wheels.

80. Attend a WaterFire Basin Lighting: New Year's Eve event.

Attending a WaterFire Basin Lighting: New Year's Eve event in Providence promises a uniquely enchanting way to welcome the new year. WaterFire, known for its mesmerizing bonfire installations on the city's waterways, transforms into a magical spectacle during this special occasion, combining the festive spirit of New Year's Eve with the signature artistry of WaterFire.

As you gather along the riverbanks to witness the basin lighting, you'll likely be surrounded by a vibrant and celebratory atmosphere. The flickering flames reflected on the water create a stunning visual display, setting the stage for an unforgettable New Year's Eve experience.

The event often includes live performances, music, and entertainment that add to the festive ambiance. The surrounding area may be adorned with festive decorations, and the air is filled with the excitement and anticipation of the upcoming countdown to midnight.

The unique combination of the basin lighting and New Year's Eve festivities provides a magical backdrop for reflection and celebration. It offers a distinctive way to bid farewell to the old year and welcome the new one, surrounded by the warmth of the bonfires and the company of fellow revelers.

Whether you choose to enjoy the event from the riverbanks, participate in nearby New Year's Eve activities, or simply take in the serene beauty of the basin lighting, attending WaterFire on New Year's Eve in Providence offers a memorable and atmospheric start to the year ahead. It's a celebration that seamlessly weaves art, community, and the spirit of the holiday season, making it a unique and cherished tradition in the city.

81. Explore the Kennedy Plaza skating rink in winter.

Exploring the Kennedy Plaza skating rink in winter is a delightful and festive experience that captures the seasonal charm of Providence. The rink, often set up during the winter months, transforms Kennedy Plaza into a winter wonderland, inviting locals and visitors to enjoy the classic pastime of ice skating amidst the city's vibrant atmosphere.

As you approach the rink, you'll likely be greeted by the joyful sounds of skates gliding across the ice and the laughter of skaters of all ages. The rink is typically adorned with twinkling lights and seasonal decorations, creating a magical ambiance that complements the winter landscape.

Whether you're an experienced skater or a novice, the Kennedy Plaza skating rink caters to all skill levels. Rental skates are usually available, allowing everyone to partake in the winter fun. The smooth ice surface, framed by the backdrop of the city, provides an idyllic setting for a day or evening of skating.

Skating at Kennedy Plaza offers more than just a recreational activity; it's an opportunity to soak in the winter spirit and enjoy the camaraderie of fellow skaters. The rink often hosts special events, such as themed skate nights or performances, adding an extra layer of entertainment to the experience.

Surrounded by the cityscape and the energy of downtown Providence, the Kennedy Plaza skating rink provides a unique blend of urban charm and winter festivity. After a joyful skate, you might find nearby cafes or vendors offering hot cocoa or seasonal treats, allowing you to warm up and extend the enjoyment of the winter outing.

Whether you're skating with family and friends, enjoying a date night, or simply relishing the winter air, the Kennedy Plaza skating rink provides a heartwarming and festive activity that contributes to the lively winter atmosphere in Providence.

82. Attend a Providence College basketball game.

Attending a Providence College basketball game is a thrilling and spirited experience that immerses you in the excitement of collegiate sports. The atmosphere at a Providence College basketball game is often charged with school spirit, fervent fan support, and the competitive energy of the players on the court.

As you step into the arena, you'll likely be greeted by the vibrant colors of the team's uniforms, the cheers of enthusiastic fans, and the rhythmic sounds of the pep band. The pre-game festivities may include performances by the cheerleading squad and the mascot, creating a dynamic and engaging environment even before the game begins.

Once the game starts, the intensity on the court and the roar of the crowd create a lively and memorable experience. Whether you're a passionate supporter of the Providence Friars or simply a fan of college basketball, the ebb and flow of the game, the strategic plays, and the thrill of each basket contribute to the overall excitement.

The Dunkin' Donuts Center, where the Providence College basketball team often plays its home games, serves as a dynamic venue that can accommodate a large and energetic crowd. The camaraderie among fans, the chants and cheers echoing through the arena, and the palpable energy make attending a game a social and communal event.

Providence College has a rich basketball tradition, and witnessing a game allows you to be a part of that tradition. Whether it's a crucial conference matchup or a heated rivalry game, the intensity and passion of the players and fans alike create an electric atmosphere that captures the essence of college basketball.

Attending a Providence College basketball game isn't just about the sport itself; it's about the sense of community, pride, and shared enthusiasm that comes with supporting the team. Win or lose, the experience of being a part of the crowd and cheering for the Friars adds to the enduring memories of college sports fandom.

83. Take a walk through the historic Smith Hill neighborhood.

Taking a walk through the historic Smith Hill neighborhood in Providence is a journey through time, offering a glimpse into the city's rich history and architectural heritage. This neighborhood, characterized by its tree-lined streets and well-preserved buildings, provides a captivating experience for those interested in exploring the historic fabric of Providence.

As you stroll through the streets of Smith Hill, you'll likely notice a mix of architectural styles that reflect different periods of the city's development. Elegant Victorian homes, colonial-era structures, and charming rowhouses contribute to the neighborhood's diverse and visually appealing character.

Travel to Providence Rhode Island

Smith Hill is home to notable landmarks such as the Rhode Island State House, a magnificent Beaux-Arts building that stands as an iconic symbol of the state's government. The State House's impressive dome and neoclassical design make it a prominent feature in the neighborhood's skyline.

Benefit Street, one of the oldest streets in Providence, extends into Smith Hill, and a walk along this historic thoroughfare reveals a treasure trove of colonial and 19th-century homes. The architecture on Benefit Street showcases the evolution of Providence over the centuries and provides a sense of the city's colonial roots.

The neighborhood is also characterized by its community-oriented atmosphere, with local parks, schools, and churches playing integral roles in the lives of residents. The Saint Patrick Church, for example, stands as a historic and cultural landmark, contributing to the neighborhood's identity.

Smith Hill's walkable streets and well-maintained sidewalks create a welcoming environment for pedestrians. Exploring the neighborhood on foot allows you to appreciate the intricate details of the historic homes, the charm of pocket parks, and the vibrant community life that defines Smith Hill.

Overall, a walk through the historic Smith Hill neighborhood is a journey that combines architectural appreciation, cultural exploration, and a connection to Providence's past. It's an opportunity to immerse yourself in the city's heritage, discover hidden gems, and enjoy the unique ambiance of one of its most historically significant districts.

84. Visit the RISD Fleet Library.

Visiting the RISD Fleet Library is a treat for those with an appreciation for art, design, and the vast world of creative expression. The Fleet Library, situated within the Rhode Island School of Design (RISD), serves as a hub of knowledge and inspiration for students, faculty, and the public alike.

Upon entering the library, you're likely to encounter a dynamic and creative environment. The Fleet Library's design reflects the innovative spirit of RISD, with open spaces, contemporary architecture, and strategically placed art installations that enhance the overall aesthetic experience.

The library is home to an extensive collection of resources, including a diverse array of books, journals, and multimedia materials that span various disciplines within the realm of art and design. Whether you're interested in visual arts, graphic design, industrial design, or any other creative field, the Fleet Library offers a treasure trove of information to explore.

One notable feature is the Materials Collection, where you can find an eclectic assortment of unconventional and traditional materials, encouraging students to experiment with textures, forms, and artistic possibilities. This hands-on approach aligns with RISD's philosophy of fostering creativity and pushing the boundaries of artistic expression.

The library's atmosphere is conducive to both focused study and collaborative work. With dedicated study spaces, computer stations, and specialized collections, it caters to the diverse needs of the RISD community. The knowledgeable library staff is often available to assist visitors in navigating the extensive collection and accessing resources relevant to their interests.

In addition to its vast collection, the Fleet Library often hosts exhibitions, events, and lectures that further contribute to the intellectual and creative vibrancy of the RISD community. Whether you're a student conducting research, an art enthusiast exploring new ideas, or a visitor seeking inspiration, the RISD Fleet Library invites you to immerse yourself in a world where art and knowledge intersect.

85. Attend a concert at the Dunkin' Donuts Center.

Attending a concert at the Dunkin' Donuts Center in Providence is an exhilarating and memorable experience that combines the thrill of live music with the energy of a large-scale venue. This multi-purpose arena serves as a premier entertainment destination, attracting a diverse range of artists and performers.

As you enter the Dunkin' Donuts Center, you'll likely be greeted by the hum of anticipation and the buzz of excitement from fellow concertgoers. The arena's modern facilities and state-of-the-art sound and lighting systems ensure that every seat offers a prime vantage point to enjoy the performance.

Travel to Providence Rhode Island

The versatility of the Dunkin' Donuts Center allows it to host a variety of concerts, from chart-topping pop acts to iconic rock bands, hip-hop artists, and more. The arena's capacity to accommodate large audiences creates a dynamic and communal atmosphere, with fans coming together to share in the experience of live music.

The stage setup and production values are often designed to enhance the visual and auditory aspects of the performance. The combination of spectacular lighting displays, high-quality acoustics, and the sheer energy of a live audience contribute to the immersive and unforgettable nature of concerts at the Dunkin' Donuts Center.

Not only does the venue provide a platform for world-renowned musicians, but it also offers a unique opportunity for local and emerging artists to showcase their talents to a broad audience.

The Dunkin' Donuts Center's central location in downtown Providence adds to the overall experience, allowing concertgoers to explore the city's vibrant nightlife, dining, and entertainment options before or after the event.

Whether you're a devoted fan of a particular artist or simply seeking an electrifying night out, attending a concert at the Dunkin' Donuts Center promises an atmosphere of celebration, musical discovery, and a shared sense of excitement that defines the magic of live performances.

86.Explore the Blackstone River Valley National Historical Park.

Exploring the Blackstone River Valley National Historical Park offers a journey through the industrial history of the United States and a chance to connect with the natural beauty of the region. Designated as a national historical park, the Blackstone River Valley preserves and interprets the story of the birth of the American Industrial Revolution.

As you venture into the park, you'll likely encounter a landscape that seamlessly blends historic sites, scenic vistas, and recreational opportunities. The Blackstone River, which played a pivotal role in the region's industrial development, flows through the park, providing a picturesque backdrop for exploration.

The historical park includes a network of sites and features that highlight the significance of the Blackstone River Valley. You may come across old mill buildings, canal remnants, and other industrial structures that once powered the early mills of the Industrial Revolution. Interpretive signs and exhibits provide insights into the technological innovations and social changes that marked this transformative period in American history.

The Blackstone River Bikeway, a multi-use path that winds its way through the park, offers a fantastic opportunity for biking, walking, or jogging. This scenic route provides access to various points of interest, allowing visitors to appreciate the historical and natural aspects of the park at their own pace.

Museum and visitor centers within the park, such as the Blackstone River Valley Visitor Center, offer additional resources to enhance your understanding of the region's history. Knowledgeable park rangers may be available to provide guided tours or answer questions, ensuring a rich and educational experience.

Throughout the park, you'll likely encounter spots ideal for picnicking, birdwatching, and enjoying the tranquil surroundings. The seasonal changes in the landscape make each visit unique, with vibrant foliage in the fall and blossoming nature in the spring.

Exploring the Blackstone River Valley National Historical Park is a chance to step back in time, appreciating the ingenuity of early American industry while immersing yourself in the scenic charm of the natural environment. It's an opportunity to connect with the roots of the nation's industrial heritage and gain a deeper appreciation for the role the Blackstone River Valley played in shaping the history of the United States.

87. Attend a WaterFire ArtMart event.

Attending a WaterFire ArtMart event in Providence offers a unique and vibrant experience, bringing together the community to celebrate local artistry in the enchanting atmosphere created by the iconic WaterFire installations. The ArtMart events, often held in conjunction with WaterFire lightings, showcase the work of talented artists and artisans in a lively and engaging marketplace setting.

As you explore the ArtMart, you'll likely encounter a diverse array of booths featuring handmade crafts, jewelry, paintings, sculptures, and other unique pieces created by local artists. The event provides a platform for artists to connect directly with the public, offering an opportunity to discuss their work, share inspirations, and forge connections with art enthusiasts.

The setting, often along the scenic riverbanks or in a designated area adjacent to the WaterFire installations, adds to the charm of the ArtMart. The flickering flames, the soothing sounds of water, and the overall ambiance contribute to a sensory-rich experience, turning the event into more than just a marketplace—it becomes a celebration of creativity and community.

Visitors to the ArtMart can expect a festive atmosphere with live performances, music, and perhaps even interactive art installations. The combination of visual and performing arts creates an immersive environment that fosters a sense of cultural appreciation and shared creativity.

These events also provide an excellent opportunity to support local artists and makers, as attendees have the chance to purchase one-of-a-kind artworks and handcrafted items directly from the creators. Whether you're looking for a unique piece to adorn your home or searching for distinctive gifts, the ArtMart offers a curated selection of items that reflect the talent and diversity of the local artistic community.

Attending a WaterFire ArtMart event becomes more than just a shopping excursion; it's a chance to engage with the arts, connect with the local creative scene, and become part of the dynamic and inclusive cultural fabric that defines Providence. It's a celebration of creativity, community, and the transformative power of art against the captivating backdrop of WaterFire.

88. Take a cruise with Save The Bay.

Embarking on a cruise with Save The Bay in Providence offers a scenic and educational journey through the picturesque waters of Narragansett Bay. Save The Bay, a nonprofit organization dedicated to the preservation and protection of Narragansett Bay, provides an opportunity for visitors to explore and appreciate the bay's natural beauty while learning about its ecosystems and environmental significance.

As you set sail, you'll likely be greeted by knowledgeable guides or naturalists who will share insights into the bay's marine life, coastal habitats, and environmental conservation efforts. The cruise may include narrated commentary that enhances the experience, providing a deeper understanding of the bay's ecology, history, and the ongoing efforts to protect its delicate balance.

The route of the cruise may take you past iconic landmarks such as lighthouses, historic forts, and picturesque coastal landscapes. You'll have the chance to witness the diverse marine life that inhabits the bay, from seabirds and seals to various fish species. The calming sound of the water and the fresh sea breeze add to the overall tranquility of the journey.

Save The Bay's commitment to environmental education often means that the cruise experience goes beyond leisure. Visitors may have the opportunity to actively participate in citizen science initiatives, such as water quality monitoring or wildlife observation, contributing to the organization's ongoing conservation efforts.

Whether you're a nature enthusiast, a family looking for an educational outing, or someone seeking a peaceful escape on the water, a cruise with Save The Bay provides a unique and enriching experience. It allows you to connect with the natural beauty of Narragansett Bay, gain insights into the region's ecology, and support the vital work of an organization dedicated to the preservation of this ecologically significant waterway.

89. Attend a performance at the Firehouse Theater.

Attending a performance at the Firehouse Theater in Providence promises an evening filled with laughter, creativity, and the unique charm of live improv and sketch comedy. The Firehouse Theater is renowned for its dynamic and entertaining shows, often featuring talented local comedians and improvisers who captivate audiences with their quick wit and comedic prowess.

Upon entering the Firehouse Theater, you'll likely be welcomed by an intimate and cozy setting that fosters a sense of connection between performers and audience members. The close proximity to the stage creates an engaging atmosphere, allowing you to feel like an active participant in the comedic experience.

The performances at the Firehouse Theater often include improv shows where the content is created on the spot based on audience suggestions. This interactive element ensures that each show is unique, and the spontaneous nature of improv adds an element of unpredictability and hilarity. The skilled comedians on stage feed off audience energy, creating a symbiotic relationship that contributes to the overall enjoyment of the performance.

In addition to improv, the Firehouse Theater may host sketch comedy shows and themed performances that showcase the versatility and creativity of the local comedy scene. Whether you're a fan of witty sketches, clever improvisation, or just looking for a night of laughter, the Firehouse Theater caters to a variety of comedic tastes.

The venue's commitment to fostering a welcoming and inclusive environment makes it an excellent choice for a night out with friends, a date, or simply for those seeking a lighthearted and entertaining experience. The Firehouse Theater stands as a hub for laughter, community, and the joy that comes from live comedic performances, making it a standout destination in Providence's vibrant arts and entertainment scene.

90. Explore the Scituate Reservoir area.

Exploring the Scituate Reservoir area provides a serene and scenic experience in a natural setting that is known for its beauty and tranquility. The Scituate Reservoir, one of the largest drinking water reservoirs in the United States, is surrounded by lush landscapes and offers opportunities for outdoor recreation and appreciation of nature.

Hiking and Nature Trails:
The reservoir area often features hiking and nature trails that allow visitors to explore the surrounding woodlands. Trails may offer varying levels of difficulty, providing options for both casual walkers and avid hikers. These trails often provide picturesque views of the reservoir and its peaceful surroundings.

Fishing:
The reservoir is a popular destination for fishing enthusiasts. The calm waters are home to various fish species, providing a tranquil setting for anglers. Make sure to check local regulations and obtain any necessary permits before fishing.

Scenic Overlooks:
Scattered around the reservoir, you may find scenic overlooks that offer panoramic views of the water and the surrounding landscape. These viewpoints provide excellent opportunities for photography and quiet contemplation.

Picnicking Areas:
Some areas around the reservoir may have designated picnicking spots. These areas are ideal for bringing a packed lunch and enjoying a meal amidst the natural beauty of the reservoir.

Birdwatching:
The reservoir and its adjacent woodlands are habitats for diverse bird species. Birdwatchers can enjoy observing local and migratory birds in their natural environment. Bring binoculars and a bird guide for an enhanced birdwatching experience.

Wildlife Observation:
Beyond birds, the reservoir area is home to various wildlife. Keep an eye out for deer, small mammals, and other creatures that inhabit the wooded areas around the reservoir.

Educational Programs:
Some reservoir areas may offer educational programs or interpretive centers that provide information about the region's ecology, the importance of water conservation, and the history of the reservoir.

Remember to respect any posted regulations and guidelines to ensure the preservation of the natural environment. Whether you're seeking outdoor activities, a peaceful retreat, or a chance to connect with nature, the Scituate Reservoir area offers a tranquil escape in the heart of Rhode Island.

91. Attend the Providence Anarchist Book Fair.

Attending the Providence Anarchist Book Fair offers a unique and thought-provoking experience for individuals interested in exploring alternative perspectives on politics, society, and activism. The book fair serves as a gathering space for anarchists, activists, and independent publishers to engage in discussions, share ideas, and showcase literature that challenges conventional notions of governance and social structures.

Book Vendors:

Travel to Providence Rhode Island

The heart of the event lies in the diverse array of book vendors and publishers who bring forth literature on anarchism, social justice, anti-authoritarianism, and related themes. The fair provides an opportunity to discover and purchase a wide range of books, zines, and publications that delve into alternative political ideologies and grassroots movements.

Workshops and Discussions:
The Providence Anarchist Book Fair typically features workshops, panel discussions, and presentations by activists, authors, and scholars. These sessions provide a platform for in-depth exploration of anarchist principles, direct action strategies, and discussions on building more equitable and inclusive communities.

Networking and Community Building:
The fair serves as a hub for like-minded individuals to connect and build networks. Attendees may include activists, anarchists, community organizers, and those interested in grassroots movements. The event fosters a sense of community and provides an opportunity to engage in meaningful conversations with people who share a passion for social change.

Art and Culture:
Beyond literature, the fair may incorporate elements of art, culture, and performance. Artistic expressions, such as visual art, music, and spoken word performances, may be integrated to complement the themes of the event.

Political Activism:
The Providence Anarchist Book Fair is often aligned with political activism. Attendees may find information on ongoing campaigns, local organizing efforts, and ways to get involved in various social justice initiatives.

Inclusivity and Diversity:
Anarchist principles often emphasize inclusivity and diversity. The book fair reflects these values by providing a platform for a variety of perspectives within the anarchist tradition, encouraging dialogue and understanding among attendees.

Attending the Providence Anarchist Book Fair is not just about acquiring books; it's a holistic experience that invites participants to engage with ideas, challenge preconceptions, and actively participate in discussions about creating a more just and equitable world.

92. Take a Providence Pedestrian Bridge walk.

Taking a walk along the Providence Pedestrian Bridge offers a delightful and scenic experience, providing panoramic views of the city, river, and surrounding landscapes. The bridge, also known as the Providence River Pedestrian Bridge, connects the East Side of Providence with downtown and serves as a picturesque pathway for pedestrians and cyclists.

Scenic Views:
As you begin your walk on the bridge, you'll be treated to stunning views of the Providence skyline, the Providence River, and Waterplace Park. The vantage point from the bridge allows for captivating photos of the cityscape, especially during sunrise or sunset.

Waterplace Park:
The bridge spans the Providence River and provides a direct link to Waterplace Park. This park features picturesque waterways, cobblestone walkways, and the iconic WaterFire installations. Taking a stroll through the park adds to the overall charm of your pedestrian bridge walk.

Riverwalk and Gondola Rides:
The bridge is part of the larger Providence Riverwalk, a scenic path along the river. While walking, you might spot gondolas gliding along the water, adding a touch of romance and elegance to the surroundings. Gondola rides are a popular activity and offer a unique perspective of the city.

Public Art and Installations:
The Providence Pedestrian Bridge often features public art installations, sculptures, and murals along its path. These artistic elements contribute to the cultural richness of the area and provide points of interest for pedestrians.

Connectivity to East Side:
The bridge serves as a vital link between the East Side neighborhoods and downtown Providence. It's a convenient route for those looking to explore both areas on foot or by bike.

Fitness and Recreation:
The bridge is a popular route for fitness enthusiasts and joggers. Its wide pathways and scenic surroundings make it an ideal location for those seeking a healthy and enjoyable outdoor exercise experience.

Events and Festivals:
Throughout the year, the bridge and its adjacent areas may host events, festivals, or markets. Checking the local events calendar might reveal opportunities to engage in community activities during your walk.

Whether you're looking for a leisurely stroll, a jog with a view, or a serene spot to enjoy the beauty of Providence, a walk across the Providence Pedestrian Bridge offers a wonderful blend of urban and natural elements in one of the city's most picturesque settings.

93. Explore the Pawtucket Arts Collaborative.

Exploring the Pawtucket Arts Collaborative provides a dynamic and enriching experience for individuals passionate about the arts and the creative community. The Pawtucket Arts Collaborative (PAC) is a non-profit organization that fosters artistic expression, collaboration, and engagement within the Pawtucket and greater Rhode Island arts scene.

Artistic Exhibitions:
PAC often hosts exhibitions featuring the works of local artists. Visiting these exhibitions provides an opportunity to discover a diverse range of artistic styles, mediums, and perspectives. The gallery spaces within the collaborative may showcase paintings, sculptures, photography, and more.

Community Engagement:
The collaborative actively engages with the local community through various art-related events, projects, and initiatives. This may include art walks, open studios, and collaborative projects that bring artists and community members together.

Artist Studios:
Some art collaboratives, including PAC, may provide studio spaces for local artists. Exploring these studios allows visitors to witness the creative process, interact with artists, and gain insight into the diverse artistic practices within the community.

Workshops and Classes:

PAC often organizes workshops and classes conducted by experienced artists. These sessions may cover a wide range of artistic techniques, providing opportunities for both aspiring and established artists to enhance their skills and knowledge.

Public Art Projects:
The collaborative may contribute to public art projects, installations, or murals that add vibrancy and cultural significance to the surrounding neighborhoods. Exploring these public art pieces becomes an integral part of the collaborative's impact on the local landscape.

Artistic Events and Performances:
PAC may host events that go beyond visual arts, including performances such as music concerts, theater productions, or spoken word performances. These events contribute to a multidisciplinary approach, showcasing the diversity of artistic expression.

Art Sales and Markets:
Collaboratives often organize art sales or markets where visitors can purchase original artworks directly from local artists. These events support the artists financially while allowing art enthusiasts to bring home unique pieces.

Networking and Collaboration:
The collaborative serves as a hub for networking and collaboration within the artistic community. Artists, art enthusiasts, and the general public can connect, share ideas, and participate in collaborative projects that contribute to the growth of the local arts scene.

Exploring the Pawtucket Arts Collaborative offers a multifaceted experience that goes beyond traditional gallery visits. It provides a glimpse into the vitality of the local arts community, encourages community participation, and celebrates the transformative power of art in enriching the cultural fabric of Pawtucket.

94. Attend a show at the Columbus Theatre.

Attending a show at the Columbus Theatre in Providence promises a unique and intimate cultural experience in a historic and beautifully restored venue. The Columbus Theatre, located on Broadway, is known for hosting a diverse range of performances, including live music, theater productions, and other artistic events.

Travel to Providence Rhode Island

Historic Architecture:
The Columbus Theatre is housed in a historic building dating back to 1926, featuring stunning Mediterranean Revival architecture. The venue itself is a work of art, with ornate detailing, arched windows, and a timeless charm that adds to the overall ambiance of the performances.

Live Music Concerts:
The theatre is renowned for its live music concerts, showcasing a variety of genres from indie and folk to rock and alternative. The intimate setting allows for a close connection between performers and the audience, creating an immersive and memorable concert experience.

Theatrical Productions:
In addition to musical performances, the Columbus Theatre often hosts theatrical productions, including plays, performances, and other live entertainment. The stage becomes a canvas for storytelling, drama, and artistic expression.

Film Screenings and Events:
The venue occasionally hosts film screenings, film festivals, and other cinematic events. The combination of a historic setting and the magic of cinema creates a unique movie-watching experience.

Acoustic Excellence:
The Columbus Theatre is known for its exceptional acoustics, providing a high-quality audio experience for both musicians and the audience. This attention to sound quality enhances the overall enjoyment of live performances.

Intimate Setting:
One of the standout features of the Columbus Theatre is its intimate setting. The relatively small seating capacity allows for a close connection between performers and the audience, creating an atmosphere of shared energy and appreciation.

Cultural and Community Events:
The theatre often serves as a venue for cultural and community events, supporting local artists and fostering a sense of community engagement. This may include art exhibitions, poetry readings, and other gatherings.

Coffee Shop Atmosphere:

The theatre's attached coffee shop, The Columbus Cooperative, provides a cozy space to grab a beverage before or after the show. It adds to the overall experience, creating a welcoming environment for patrons.

Attending a show at the Columbus Theatre is not just about the performance; it's about immersing yourself in a cultural and artistic experience within a historic and visually stunning setting. Whether you're a music lover, theatre enthusiast, or simply seeking a night of entertainment, the Columbus Theatre offers a memorable and enriching experience in the heart of Providence.

95. Take a Providence Neighborhood Plant Walk.

Taking a plant walk in the neighborhoods of Providence offers a delightful and educational experience, allowing you to discover the diverse flora that contributes to the city's greenery. Whether you're strolling through residential areas, parks, or historic districts, you'll likely encounter a variety of plants, trees, and flowers. Here's a suggested plan for a Providence neighborhood plant walk:

Choose a Neighborhood:
Select a neighborhood in Providence that interests you. Each neighborhood has its own character and green spaces, such as College Hill, Federal Hill, or the East Side.

Parks and Gardens:
Start your walk in a local park or community garden. Providence is home to several beautiful parks, such as Roger Williams Park, Waterplace Park, and Prospect Terrace Park. These spaces often feature well-maintained gardens and a diverse range of plants.

Historic Districts:
Explore historic districts like College Hill, where you'll find tree-lined streets with historic homes and a mix of native and ornamental plants. Benefit Street, known for its historic architecture, is particularly charming.

Botanical Points of Interest:
Identify any botanical points of interest in the neighborhood. This might include notable trees, public gardens, or green spaces maintained by community groups.

Travel to Providence Rhode Island

Local Flora:
Observe the local flora as you walk. Take note of the types of trees, shrubs, and flowers you encounter. Some neighborhoods may have community gardens where residents cultivate a variety of plants.

Street Trees:
Pay attention to the trees planted along the streets. Many cities, including Providence, have urban forestry programs that aim to enhance the urban environment through strategic tree planting.

Public Spaces:
Explore public spaces such as squares or plazas. These areas often feature landscaping and plantings that contribute to the aesthetics of the neighborhood.

Botanical Identification:
If you're interested in plant identification, bring along a field guide or use a plant identification app to learn more about the plants you encounter.

Seasonal Variations:
Keep in mind that the plant landscape can vary with the seasons. Spring and summer bring vibrant blooms, while fall showcases foliage colors.

Respect Nature:
As you enjoy the plant walk, be respectful of private property and nature. Avoid picking flowers or damaging plants, and stay on designated paths.

Taking a plant walk in Providence's neighborhoods provides an opportunity to connect with nature, appreciate the city's green spaces, and gain insights into the local flora. Enjoy the beauty of the plants while exploring the diverse and vibrant neighborhoods of Providence.

96. Visit the Pawtucket Wintertime Farmers Market.

Visiting the Pawtucket Wintertime Farmers Market is a wonderful way to experience the local flavors, crafts, and community spirit during the winter months. The Pawtucket Wintertime Farmers Market is known for featuring a variety of vendors offering fresh produce, artisanal products, and handmade crafts. Here's what you might expect during your visit:

Fresh Produce and Local Goods:
Explore the stalls of local farmers and producers offering fresh, seasonal produce, dairy products, meats, and more. The market is an excellent place to source high-quality ingredients for your meals and support local agriculture.

Artisanal Foods:
Discover a diverse range of artisanal and specialty foods. From baked goods and jams to cheeses and prepared meals, the market showcases the creativity and culinary expertise of local producers.

Handmade Crafts:
Many wintertime markets also feature local artisans and crafters. You may find unique handmade items such as pottery, jewelry, textiles, and other crafts, making it a great place to shop for gifts or souvenirs.

Warm Beverages:
Winter markets often offer warm beverages to keep visitors cozy. Look out for vendors selling hot coffee, tea, cocoa, or other seasonal drinks.

Live Entertainment:
Some markets incorporate live music or entertainment, creating a festive and enjoyable atmosphere for visitors. Check the market's schedule for any planned performances or activities.

Community Engagement:
Farmers markets are community hubs, and the wintertime market in Pawtucket is likely to foster a sense of community engagement. You may have the chance to meet local farmers, artisans, and fellow residents.

Seasonal Decor and Plants:
Explore seasonal decorations and plants that can add a touch of winter charm to your home. Vendors may offer wreaths, poinsettias, and other festive items.

Cooking Demonstrations:
Some markets feature cooking demonstrations where local chefs showcase recipes using ingredients available at the market. This can provide inspiration for preparing seasonal dishes at home.

Kid-Friendly Activities:
Family-friendly markets often include activities for children. Look for face painting, storytelling sessions, or other kid-friendly attractions.

Check Market Hours:
Before planning your visit, check the market's hours of operation. Wintertime markets may have specific schedules, and it's always a good idea to arrive early for the best selection.

Remember to bring a reusable bag to carry your purchases, and consider checking the market's website or contacting organizers for any specific guidelines or special events happening during your visit. Enjoy the vibrant and cozy atmosphere of the Pawtucket Wintertime Farmers Market!

97. Explore the Washington Secondary Bike Path.

Exploring the Washington Secondary Bike Path provides a scenic and recreational journey through Rhode Island's landscapes. The Washington Secondary Bike Path is a rail-trail that spans approximately 19 miles, offering a multi-use path for cyclists, walkers, and joggers. Here's a guide to your exploration:

Starting Point:
Choose a starting point for your bike ride. The Washington Secondary Bike Path extends from Cranston to Coventry, passing through various towns and natural areas.

Cranston Section:
If you start in Cranston, you'll find the path begins near the western end of the Cranston Street Armory. This section takes you through urban and suburban landscapes before transitioning into more rural scenery.

Scenic Landscapes:
As you ride along the path, you'll encounter diverse landscapes, including woodlands, wetlands, and open fields. The trail provides a mix of natural beauty and glimpses of Rhode Island's countryside.

Flat and Paved Surface:
The bike path is known for its flat and well-paved surface, making it suitable for cyclists of various skill levels. The smooth path allows for a comfortable and enjoyable ride.

Historic Features:
Keep an eye out for any historic features along the trail. Rail-trails often follow former railroad routes, and you might come across remnants of rail infrastructure or other historical points of interest.

Water Crossings:
The path crosses over several bodies of water, including rivers and streams. These crossings offer scenic views and a chance to appreciate the waterways of the region.

Rest Areas and Parks:
Look for rest areas or parks along the way. Some sections may have benches, picnic areas, or interpretive signs providing information about the natural and cultural history of the area.

Connect to Other Trails:
The Washington Secondary Bike Path connects to other trails, providing opportunities for longer rides or exploration of adjacent areas. Check trail maps to discover additional routes you might want to explore.

Cyclist-Friendly Communities:
As you pass through different towns, you'll find cyclist-friendly communities. Some areas may have bike shops, cafes, or other amenities catering to those enjoying the bike path.

Seasonal Considerations:
Be mindful of seasonal considerations. The path is enjoyable year-round, but Rhode Island's weather can vary, so come prepared with appropriate gear. Fall offers beautiful foliage, while spring and summer provide lush greenery.

Remember to adhere to trail rules and etiquette, share the path with other users, and enjoy the natural beauty and recreational opportunities that the Washington Secondary Bike Path offers. Whether you're a seasoned cyclist or a casual rider, this trail provides a pleasant escape into Rhode Island's scenic landscapes.

Travel to Providence Rhode Island

98. Attend a performance at the Providence Ballet Theatre.

Attending a performance at the Providence Ballet Theatre promises an enchanting and artistic experience, showcasing the beauty and grace of ballet. The Providence Ballet Theatre is dedicated to promoting and preserving the art of ballet through professional productions and educational programs. Here's what you can anticipate when attending a performance at the Providence Ballet Theatre:

Artistic Excellence:
The Providence Ballet Theatre is known for its commitment to artistic excellence. Performances feature highly trained and skilled dancers who bring precision, emotion, and artistry to their interpretations of classical and contemporary ballet works.

Diverse Repertoire:
Ballet performances at the Providence Ballet Theatre often encompass a diverse repertoire. This may include classical ballets such as "Swan Lake" or "The Nutcracker," as well as contemporary pieces that showcase the versatility and innovation of ballet as an art form.

Choreographic Innovation:
The theater may present works by renowned choreographers or showcase original choreography created by the artistic team. Expect to witness choreographic innovation that pushes the boundaries of classical ballet and explores new expressions of movement.

Costume and Set Design:
Productions at the Providence Ballet Theatre pay attention to visual aesthetics. Lavish costumes and carefully designed sets enhance the overall theatrical experience, transporting the audience into the magical worlds created by each ballet.

Live Music Accompaniment:
Some performances may feature live music accompaniment, adding an extra layer of richness to the ballet experience. Live orchestration enhances the connection between the music and the dancers, creating a more immersive atmosphere.

Educational and Outreach Programs:

The Providence Ballet Theatre often engages in educational and outreach programs. This may include opportunities for community involvement, school performances, and dance education initiatives to nurture a love for ballet within the broader community.

Intimate Theater Setting:
The theater may offer an intimate setting, allowing the audience to feel close to the performers and fully appreciate the nuances of the dance. The proximity enhances the emotional impact of the ballet.

Special Performances and Events:
Keep an eye out for special performances or events hosted by the Providence Ballet Theatre. This may include gala performances, fundraising events, or collaborations with other arts organizations in the community.

Before planning your visit, check the Providence Ballet Theatre's official website or contact the theater directly for information about upcoming performances, ticket availability, and any special events. Attending a ballet performance at the Providence Ballet Theatre is a cultural experience that celebrates the beauty, athleticism, and storytelling prowess of this timeless art form.

99. Take a food tour of Federal Hill.

Embarking on a food tour of Federal Hill in Providence promises a delectable journey through one of the city's most vibrant and historically rich neighborhoods. Federal Hill is renowned for its Italian-American heritage and is often referred to as Providence's Little Italy. Here's a suggested guide for your Federal Hill food tour:

Start with Pastries at a Bakery:
Begin your culinary adventure with a visit to one of Federal Hill's authentic Italian bakeries. Indulge in freshly baked pastries, cannoli, sfogliatella, or biscotti accompanied by a cup of espresso.

Explore Italian Markets:
Wander through the neighborhood's Italian markets to discover a variety of imported cheeses, cured meats, and specialty ingredients. Engage with local vendors and perhaps pick up some unique items to take home.

Travel to Providence Rhode Island

Antipasto Platter at a Trattoria:
Head to a traditional trattoria for an antipasto platter featuring an assortment of Italian cured meats, cheeses, olives, and marinated vegetables. Pair this with a glass of wine for an authentic taste of Italy.

Pasta Feast:
Federal Hill is known for its exceptional pasta dishes. Choose a restaurant that specializes in pasta and savor classics like spaghetti Bolognese, fettuccine Alfredo, or homemade lasagna.

Seafood Delicacies:
Given Providence's coastal location, explore seafood options. Enjoy a dish featuring fresh local catches, perhaps in the form of seafood risotto, clams casino, or grilled calamari.

Pizza Experience:
No food tour is complete without trying pizza. Federal Hill offers excellent pizzerias where you can savor a slice or a whole pie with various toppings.

Espresso and Gelato Break:
Take a break with a traditional Italian espresso at a local café. Pair it with a scoop of authentic gelato in a variety of flavors, providing a refreshing interlude to your savory journey.

Wine Tasting:
Explore a wine bar or enoteca to sample Italian wines. Federal Hill has establishments with extensive wine lists, allowing you to enjoy regional wines paired with your culinary choices.

Cannoli for Dessert:
Conclude your food tour with a visit to a pastry shop for a classic cannoli. Federal Hill is known for its delightful cannoli, and each bakery may have its own unique twist on this iconic treat.

After Dinner Digestif:
Wrap up your Federal Hill food tour with a digestif at a local bar or lounge. Sip on limoncello or amaro to conclude your culinary adventure.

Remember to check the operating hours and any reservation requirements for the establishments you plan to visit. Federal Hill's culinary scene is rich and diverse, offering a delightful array of Italian-inspired flavors for every palate. Enjoy your food tour through this gastronomic gem in Providence!

100. Explore the Neutaconkanut Hill Conservancy.

Exploring the Neutaconkanut Hill Conservancy provides a serene and scenic outdoor experience in the heart of Providence. Neutaconkanut Hill is a natural area that offers hiking trails, wildlife observation, and panoramic views of the surrounding landscape. Here's a guide to help you make the most of your visit:

Trailhead Exploration:
Begin your adventure at one of the trailheads. Neutaconkanut Hill Conservancy offers several trail options of varying lengths and difficulty levels, so choose one that suits your preferences and fitness level.

Hiking Amidst Nature:
Immerse yourself in nature as you hike through wooded areas, meadows, and along well-maintained trails. Keep an eye out for native flora and fauna that thrive in this urban oasis.

Scenic Overlooks:
Neutaconkanut Hill is renowned for its scenic overlooks. Reach the summit to enjoy breathtaking panoramic views of Providence, the nearby communities, and, on clear days, even distant landmarks.

Wildlife Observation:
The conservancy is home to a variety of wildlife. Bring binoculars if you're interested in birdwatching, as the hill is frequented by a diverse range of bird species. You might also encounter small mammals and other critters along the trails.

Historical Exploration:
Neutaconkanut Hill has a rich history. Explore any historical markers or remnants that provide insights into the area's past. Some trails may pass by old structures or points of interest.

Family-Friendly Activities:
If you're visiting with family, consider exploring the trails suitable for all ages. The conservancy offers a family-friendly environment, making it a great destination for a nature outing with children.

Photography Opportunities:
Capture the beauty of Neutaconkanut Hill with your camera or smartphone. The changing seasons, vibrant foliage, and the diverse landscapes provide excellent photo opportunities.

Seasonal Considerations:
Be mindful of seasonal changes. Different times of the year offer unique experiences, from vibrant spring blooms to colorful fall foliage. Winter can transform the landscape into a serene, snow-covered wonderland.

Trail Etiquette:
Follow trail etiquette by staying on designated paths, respecting wildlife, and leaving no trace. This ensures that the natural beauty of Neutaconkanut Hill is preserved for future visitors.

Check for Events or Programs:
Keep an eye on the conservancy's website for any scheduled events, guided hikes, or educational programs. Participating in organized activities can enhance your understanding of the hill's ecology and history.

Before you embark on your exploration, check trail maps, park regulations, and any seasonal considerations on the Neutaconkanut Hill Conservancy's official website. Whether you're seeking a peaceful nature walk or a more challenging hike, Neutaconkanut Hill offers a tranquil escape within the urban landscape of Providence.

101. Attend a Providence Gay Men's Chorus concert.

Attending a Providence Gay Men's Chorus concert promises an uplifting and culturally enriching experience. The Providence Gay Men's Chorus (PGMC) is known for its commitment to musical excellence, diversity, and inclusivity Here's what you can anticipate when attending one of their concerts:

Diverse Repertoire:
The PGMC often performs a diverse repertoire that spans various musical genres and styles. From classical and traditional choral pieces to contemporary and popular songs, their concerts showcase the versatility of the chorus.

Celebration of LGBTQ+ Culture:
As a LGBTQ+ chorus, the performances often celebrate LGBTQ+ culture and history. Expect to hear songs that resonate with the LGBTQ+ community and highlight themes of love, acceptance, and resilience.

Artistic Excellence:
The Providence Gay Men's Chorus is dedicated to achieving artistic excellence. The members' passion for music and commitment to their craft result in powerful and emotionally resonant performances.

Inclusive Atmosphere:
Concerts by the PGMC provide an inclusive and welcoming atmosphere for all audience members. It's a space where diversity is celebrated, and the chorus aims to create a sense of community through the power of music.

Collaborations and Special Guests:
The chorus may collaborate with other artists or feature special guests, adding a dynamic element to their performances. Keep an eye out for announcements about any notable collaborations in the concert you plan to attend.

Community Engagement:
The PGMC is actively involved in the local community. Concerts may include outreach initiatives, partnerships with LGBTQ+ organizations, or efforts to raise awareness about social issues through music.

Emotional Impact:
Choral music has a unique ability to convey emotion and connect with audiences on a deep level. Prepare to be moved by the power and beauty of the chorale arrangements.

Ticket Information:
Check the PGMC's official website or contact the chorus directly for information about ticket prices, availability, and any special considerations. Purchasing tickets in advance is advisable, especially for popular performances.

Venue Atmosphere:
Consider the venue where the concert is taking place. Whether it's a theater, concert hall, or community space, each venue contributes to the overall atmosphere of the performance.

Engage with the Chorus:

If there are opportunities for audience engagement, take advantage of them. Some concerts may include Q&A sessions, post-concert receptions, or chances to meet and interact with chorus members.

Attending a Providence Gay Men's Chorus concert not only offers an enjoyable musical experience but also contributes to the celebration of diversity and the LGBTQ+ community. Check the chorus's schedule, mark the date of the next concert, and prepare to be part of a moving and inspiring musical celebration.

102. Take a scenic drive through Foster, Rhode Island.

A scenic drive through Foster, Rhode Island promises a tranquil journey through picturesque landscapes and charming rural settings. Foster is known for its scenic beauty, historic sites, and a laid-back atmosphere. Here's a suggested route for a scenic drive through Foster:

Start in the Village of Foster:
Begin your scenic drive in the village center of Foster. Explore the historic district and take note of the quaint architecture and local charm. Foster's village area is small but offers a glimpse into the town's history.

Foster Center Historic District:
Drive through the Foster Center Historic District, where you'll find well-preserved buildings dating back to the 18th and 19th centuries. Enjoy the peaceful ambiance of this historic area.

Head North on Route 94:
Take Route 94 (Danielson Pike) northward. This route will lead you through scenic countryside with rolling hills, open fields, and wooded areas. The drive offers a mix of farmland and natural beauty.

Nichols Corner:
As you continue on Route 94, you'll pass through Nichols Corner, a charming crossroads with a rural character. Take in the scenic views of farmland and enjoy the peaceful ambiance of the area.

Stop at Local Farms:
Foster is known for its farms and agricultural activities. Consider stopping at a local farm stand or market to pick up fresh produce or other local goods.

Explore Local Roads:
Foster has a network of local roads that meander through the countryside. Consider taking some detours onto these roads to explore hidden gems and discover unexpected scenic spots.

Ponaganset Reservoir:
Head towards the Ponaganset Reservoir. The reservoir offers beautiful views and, if accessible, a peaceful place to stop and enjoy the scenery. Please be mindful of private property and follow any posted regulations.

Continue on Scenic Routes:
Explore other scenic routes in Foster, such as East Killingly Road or Howard Hill Road. These roads provide a more intimate connection with Foster's natural beauty.

Experience Seasonal Changes:
Depending on the time of year, Foster's landscape can change dramatically. Enjoy the vibrant colors of fall foliage, the blooming flowers in spring, or the quiet beauty of winter.

Foster Town Forest:
Consider a visit to the Foster Town Forest if you're interested in a short nature walk. The forest features trails and is a peaceful retreat for nature enthusiasts.

Remember to drive safely, especially on the local roads, and respect the privacy of residents and the natural environment. A scenic drive through Foster allows you to appreciate the simple beauty of rural Rhode Island and experience the town's unique character.

103.Attend a WaterFire Clear Currents: A Symposium on WaterFire event.

Attending a WaterFire Clear Currents: A Symposium on WaterFire event promises an engaging and enlightening experience focused on the intersection of art, culture, and the transformative power of water. WaterFire, a renowned public art installation in Providence, often hosts events like Clear Currents to explore themes related to its mission. Here's what you can expect:

Travel to Providence Rhode Island

In-Depth Discussions:
Clear Currents: A Symposium on WaterFire is likely to feature in-depth discussions on the various aspects of WaterFire, including its artistic elements, cultural impact, and the role of water in shaping the experience.

Artistic Insights:
Gain insights into the artistic vision behind WaterFire. The symposium may include presentations or panel discussions with artists, creators, and curators involved in the development and execution of WaterFire installations.

Cultural Significance:
Explore the cultural significance of WaterFire within the context of Providence and beyond. Learn about the historical and social aspects that contribute to WaterFire's role as a dynamic and transformative cultural event.

Interactive Sessions:
Engage in interactive sessions that may include Q&A sessions, workshops, or opportunities to participate in discussions. This allows attendees to actively contribute to the dialogue surrounding WaterFire.

Water and Environmental Themes:
Given WaterFire's connection to water and its location along the rivers of Providence, the symposium may delve into environmental themes. Expect discussions on the importance of water, sustainability, and the environmental impact of public art installations.

Networking Opportunities:
Connect with fellow attendees, artists, scholars, and enthusiasts who share an interest in the intersection of art and water. Networking opportunities can provide valuable insights and foster collaborative discussions.

Visual Presentations:
Visual presentations, such as slideshows or videos, may be incorporated to showcase the visual aspects of WaterFire. This could include behind-the-scenes footage, artistic processes, and the visual impact of the installations.

Community Engagement:
WaterFire events often emphasize community engagement. The symposium may explore how WaterFire contributes to community building, local pride, and the overall sense of belonging in Providence.

Event Logistics:

Check the event logistics, including the schedule, venue details, and any registration requirements. Planning ahead ensures that you have a seamless and enjoyable experience during the symposium.

Artistic Performances:
Some WaterFire events include artistic performances as part of the symposium. This could involve live music, dance, or other performances that enhance the overall artistic and cultural experience.

To stay updated on upcoming WaterFire events, including Clear Currents: A Symposium on WaterFire, visit the official WaterFire Providence website or contact the WaterFire office directly. Attending such a symposium offers a unique opportunity to deepen your understanding of the artistic and cultural significance of WaterFire in the vibrant city of Providence.

104. Explore the North Burial Ground.

Exploring the North Burial Ground in Providence provides not only a historical perspective but also an opportunity to appreciate the peaceful and well-maintained grounds. Here's a guide to help you make the most of your visit:

Historical Overview:
The North Burial Ground, established in 1700, holds a rich history. As one of the oldest cemeteries in Providence, it serves as the final resting place for numerous individuals, including notable figures from the city's past.

Architectural Features:
Wander through the cemetery to discover a variety of architectural features on tombstones and monuments. Some markers may showcase intricate carvings and designs, reflecting the artistry of different eras.

Notable Graves:
The cemetery is the resting place of several notable individuals, including political figures, military veterans, and community leaders. Look for markers that provide information about the historical significance of certain graves.

Veterans' Section:
Pay your respects at the veterans' section, where many soldiers from various wars are buried. The cemetery often honors military personnel with specific memorial features.

Travel to Providence Rhode Island

Botanical Diversity:
Appreciate the botanical diversity within the cemetery. Many mature trees and plantings add to the serene atmosphere, creating a peaceful environment for contemplation.

Walking Trails:
The North Burial Ground features walking trails that weave through the cemetery, allowing visitors to explore its different sections. Walking the paths provides an opportunity for quiet reflection and appreciation of the surroundings.

Cultural Preservation:
Take note of efforts made for cultural preservation within the cemetery. Preservation initiatives often aim to maintain the historical integrity of the burial ground while ensuring a respectful and well-maintained environment.

Seasonal Changes:
Consider visiting during different seasons to witness the changing landscape. Spring may bring blooming flowers, while autumn showcases the vibrant colors of fall foliage. Winter provides a different, more serene atmosphere.

Guided Tours:
Check if the cemetery offers guided tours. A knowledgeable guide can provide additional insights into the history, architecture, and stories behind the graves, enhancing your overall experience.

Photography Opportunities:
Capture the unique features and peaceful ambiance of the North Burial Ground through photography. Remember to do so with respect and sensitivity to the sacred nature of the site.

Visitor Information:
Check for any visitor information or brochures available at the entrance. These materials may offer maps, historical context, and other helpful details to enhance your self-guided exploration.

Respectful Visitation:
When exploring, maintain a respectful demeanor. Refrain from touching or leaning on tombstones, and be mindful of any posted rules or guidelines.

Visiting the North Burial Ground provides a meaningful and contemplative experience, allowing you to connect with the history of Providence and pay homage to those who have contributed to the community over the centuries.

105. Visit the Slater Mill Historic Site.

Visiting the Slater Mill Historic Site in Pawtucket, Rhode Island, offers a fascinating journey into the birthplace of the American Industrial Revolution. Here's a guide to help you make the most of your visit:

Historical Significance:
Slater Mill is historically significant as the first successful cotton-spinning factory in the United States. It played a pivotal role in the early industrialization of America.

Guided Tours:
Consider taking a guided tour of the mill. Knowledgeable guides provide insights into the history of Slater Mill, its machinery, and the impact it had on the industrial landscape of the country.

Mill Complex:
Explore the mill complex, which includes Slater Mill, the Sylvanus Brown House, and the Wilkinson Mill. Each building contributes to the overall narrative of industrial innovation and early manufacturing.

Machinery Exhibits:
Inside Slater Mill, you'll find exhibits showcasing the original machinery used in cotton spinning. Learn about Samuel Slater's innovative techniques and how they transformed the textile industry.

Sylvanus Brown House:
Visit the Sylvanus Brown House, an early 18th-century house that provides a glimpse into domestic life during the industrialization era. The house is part of the Slater Mill complex.

Wilkinson Mill:
Explore the Wilkinson Mill, adjacent to Slater Mill, which houses a machine shop and the Wilkinson Cotton Mill. Gain an understanding of the industrial processes that contributed to the success of Slater Mill.

Travel to Providence Rhode Island

Visitor Center:
Start your visit at the visitor center, where you can gather information, purchase tickets, and learn more about the exhibits and programs offered at Slater Mill Historic Site.

Educational Programs:
Check for any educational programs or events taking place during your visit. Slater Mill often hosts workshops, demonstrations, and special events related to the history of the site.

Outdoor Spaces:
Enjoy the outdoor spaces around the mill complex. The site is situated along the Blackstone River, providing a picturesque setting for a leisurely stroll.

Blackstone River Greenway:
Take advantage of the proximity to the Blackstone River Greenway. Consider exploring this scenic walking and biking path that runs alongside the river and offers beautiful views.

Gift Shop:
Visit the gift shop for souvenirs, books, and other items related to the history of Slater Mill and the Industrial Revolution.

Plan Your Visit:
Before your visit, check the Slater Mill Historic Site's official website for information on operating hours, admission fees, and any special events. Planning ahead ensures a smooth and enjoyable experience.

Visiting Slater Mill Historic Site provides a unique opportunity to connect with the roots of American industrialization and appreciate the technological advancements that shaped the nation's history.

106. Attend the Gaspee Days Parade.

Attending the Gaspee Days Parade is a lively and patriotic experience that commemorates the events leading up to the American Revolution and celebrates the spirit of freedom. Here's what you can expect when participating in the Gaspee Days Parade:

Historical Significance:

The Gaspee Days Parade commemorates the burning of the HMS Gaspee in 1772, a key event that contributed to the lead-up to the American Revolution. The parade honors this historical moment and the spirit of resistance against British authority.

Patriotic Atmosphere:
Immerse yourself in a patriotic atmosphere as the parade showcases a display of American pride, with participants often dressed in colonial-era costumes, military uniforms, and patriotic colors.

Marching Bands and Musical Performances:
Enjoy the energetic performances of marching bands, fife and drum corps, and musical groups that contribute to the festive ambiance of the parade. The music often reflects the historical period and adds to the overall experience.

Floats and Decorations:
The parade features creatively decorated floats that depict scenes from American history, paying homage to the nation's heritage and the ideals of freedom and independence.

Community Involvement:
Gaspee Days Parade is a community-driven event, with local organizations, schools, and community groups participating. It provides an opportunity for residents to come together and celebrate their shared history and values.

Historical Reenactments:
Some parades may include historical reenactments, bringing to life the events surrounding the Gaspee Affair. These reenactments offer educational insights into the challenges faced by early American colonists.

Family-Friendly Activities:
The Gaspee Days Parade is often family-friendly, with activities and entertainment suitable for all ages. Children and adults alike can enjoy the festive atmosphere and learn more about American history.

Street Performers and Entertainers:
Look out for street performers, entertainers, and characters that add an element of fun and excitement to the parade route. These individuals often interact with the crowd, enhancing the overall experience.

Local Vendors and Food Stalls:

Explore local vendors and food stalls that may be set up along the parade route. It's an opportunity to sample local cuisine, enjoy snacks, and support small businesses in the community.

Parade Route and Viewing Areas:
Check the parade route in advance and find a comfortable spot to view the procession. Arrive early to secure a good vantage point and to fully enjoy the festivities.

Community Spirit:
Experience the strong sense of community spirit as residents come together to celebrate their shared history and values. The Gaspee Days Parade fosters a sense of pride and unity among participants and spectators alike.

Plan Ahead:
Plan your visit by checking the official Gaspee Days Parade website or contacting local event organizers for information on the schedule, parking, and any specific guidelines for attendees.

Attending the Gaspee Days Parade is not just a celebration of history but also a chance to embrace the community's spirit and patriotism. Be prepared for an engaging and festive experience that honors the legacy of those who played a role in shaping the nation's history.

107. Take a stroll through DePasquale Square.

Taking a stroll through DePasquale Square in Providence, specifically located in the Federal Hill neighborhood, offers a charming and vibrant experience. Here's a guide to help you make the most of your leisurely walk through this lively square:

Italian Heritage:
DePasquale Square is at the heart of Federal Hill, the city's Little Italy. Immerse yourself in the rich Italian heritage of the area, evident in the architecture, signage, and overall ambiance.

Outdoor Seating and Cafes:

Explore the various cafes and restaurants that offer outdoor seating in the square. Enjoy a leisurely coffee or a meal while observing the lively atmosphere around you.

Piazza-Style Setting:
Experience the piazza-style setting of DePasquale Square. The design of the square, with its fountain and open spaces, encourages a relaxed and social environment.

Seasonal Decorations:
Depending on the time of year, you may encounter seasonal decorations and events in the square. Federal Hill is known for its festive atmosphere during holidays and special occasions.

Local Shops and Boutiques:
Wander into the local shops and boutiques surrounding the square. Explore unique finds, Italian specialties, and artisan goods that contribute to the area's character.

Historic Architecture:
Take note of the historic architecture that surrounds the square. Federal Hill features a mix of historic buildings, each with its own story and charm.

Fountain and Public Art:
Appreciate the central fountain in the square, a focal point that adds to the aesthetic appeal. Look for any public art installations that may enhance the cultural and artistic atmosphere.

Live Entertainment:
Check if there are any live entertainment or events taking place in DePasquale Square. The area is known for hosting outdoor concerts, festivals, and other community gatherings.

People-Watching:
Find a comfortable spot and engage in some people-watching. DePasquale Square attracts a diverse mix of locals and visitors, providing an excellent opportunity for observation.

Italian Markets:

If there are Italian markets or grocery stores nearby, consider exploring them. You might discover authentic ingredients, specialty foods, and unique products that reflect the Italian culinary tradition.

Bakeries and Gelato Shops:
Indulge your sweet tooth by visiting local bakeries and gelato shops. Federal Hill is renowned for its delicious pastries, cannoli, and other Italian treats.

Community Events:
Stay informed about any community events or activities happening in DePasquale Square. These events can range from cultural celebrations to art exhibitions and contribute to the square's dynamic atmosphere.

A stroll through DePasquale Square is not just a walk; it's an immersion into the cultural and culinary delights of Federal Hill. Whether you're savoring Italian cuisine, enjoying outdoor seating, or simply taking in the sights and sounds, the square offers a delightful experience in the heart of Providence.

108. Explore the Slater Park Zoo in Pawtucket.

Exploring Slater Park Zoo in Pawtucket provides a wonderful opportunity to connect with wildlife, enjoy outdoor spaces, and learn about conservation efforts. Here's a guide to help you make the most of your visit:

Animal Exhibits:
Begin your visit by exploring the various animal exhibits at Slater Park Zoo. From native species to exotic animals, the zoo offers a diverse range of wildlife to observe and learn about.

Red Wolf Breeding Program:
Learn about the zoo's involvement in the Red Wolf Species Survival Plan. Slater Park Zoo has been actively participating in the breeding program for this critically endangered species.

Interactive Exhibits:
Look for interactive exhibits that provide hands-on learning experiences. Some exhibits may allow visitors to get closer to certain animals and engage in educational activities.

Waterfowl Aviary:
Explore the Waterfowl Aviary, which is home to a variety of water-loving birds. Enjoy the tranquil setting and observe the different species of ducks and other waterfowl.

Walk Through the Zoo:
Take your time walking through the zoo, enjoying the landscaped pathways and greenery. Many exhibits are designed to mimic natural habitats, providing a more immersive experience.

Children's Exploration Zone:
If you're visiting with children, check out the Children's Exploration Zone. This area often includes interactive play spaces and exhibits designed for younger visitors.

Educational Programs:
Inquire about any educational programs or animal demonstrations taking place during your visit. Zookeepers may offer talks or demonstrations to provide additional insights into the animals and conservation efforts.

Picnic Areas:
Slater Park Zoo is located within Slater Memorial Park, which offers picturesque picnic areas. Consider bringing a picnic lunch to enjoy in the park after your zoo visit.

Seasonal Events:
Check the zoo's calendar for any seasonal events or special programs. Many zoos host events during holidays or specific times of the year, providing additional entertainment and educational opportunities.

Gift Shop:
Visit the zoo's gift shop for souvenirs and educational materials. Purchasing items from the gift shop often contributes to the zoo's conservation efforts.

Photography Opportunities:
Capture memories by taking photographs of the animals and the beautiful surroundings. Be mindful of any guidelines regarding photography within the zoo.

Plan Your Visit:

Travel to Providence Rhode Island

Check the zoo's official website for information on hours of operation, admission fees, and any COVID-related guidelines. Planning ahead ensures a smooth and enjoyable visit.

Slater Park Zoo provides a family-friendly and educational experience, making it an excellent destination for nature enthusiasts, families, and anyone interested in wildlife conservation. Enjoy your time exploring the zoo and connecting with the fascinating world of animals.

109. Attend a WaterFire Tribute to the Olympics event.

Attending a WaterFire Tribute to the Olympics event promises a unique and captivating experience, blending the enchanting atmosphere of WaterFire with the spirit of the Olympic Games. Here's what you can expect during this special event:

Luminous WaterFire Installation:
Witness the iconic WaterFire installation, where a series of braziers are lit along the rivers, creating a mesmerizing display of light on the water. The flames, set against the backdrop of the night sky, evoke a sense of enchantment.

Olympic Theme:
The event pays tribute to the Olympics, incorporating thematic elements that celebrate the international spirit of the Games. Look out for symbolic decorations, colors, and perhaps even Olympic-themed performances.

Symbolic Lighting Ceremonies:
WaterFire events often feature symbolic lighting ceremonies. In the context of a Tribute to the Olympics, these ceremonies may be inspired by Olympic traditions, creating a unique fusion of cultural celebrations.

Live Performances:
Enjoy live performances that reflect the diversity of Olympic cultures. Music, dance, or theatrical acts may take center stage, adding an extra layer of entertainment to the event.

Cultural Exhibitions:

Explore cultural exhibitions or displays that highlight the global nature of the Olympics. This could include art installations, exhibits, or informational displays about different countries and their Olympic histories.

Athlete Recognitions:
As part of the tribute, there may be recognitions or acknowledgments of local athletes, Olympians, or individuals who have made significant contributions to sports and the community.

Community Involvement:
WaterFire events often emphasize community involvement. You may find opportunities to participate in interactive activities, engage with local organizations, or learn more about the cultural significance of the Olympics.

Food and Beverage Offerings:
Check for special food and beverage offerings that complement the Olympic theme. Local vendors may provide diverse culinary experiences, allowing you to savor flavors from around the world.

Thematic Art Installations:
Keep an eye out for thematic art installations that enhance the visual appeal of the event. These could include sculptures, installations, or projections that tie into the Olympic theme.

Fire Dancers or Performers:
WaterFire events occasionally feature fire dancers or performers. In the context of a Tribute to the Olympics, these performers may incorporate elements inspired by the athleticism and energy of Olympic sports.

Photography Opportunities:
Capture the magic of the event through photography. The combination of firelight, cultural displays, and live performances offers ample opportunities for striking and memorable shots.

Community Celebration:
Embrace the sense of community celebration as you join fellow attendees in commemorating the Olympics. Share in the collective joy, appreciation for cultural diversity, and the spirit of competition and unity.

Before attending, check the official WaterFire Providence website or local event listings for specific details about the Tribute to the Olympics event, including the schedule, participating performers, and any additional activities planned for the celebration. Enjoy the magical fusion of WaterFire and Olympic inspiration during this special tribute event.

110. Take a day trip to Providence Plantations.

Taking a day trip to Providence Plantations offers a chance to explore the historical and cultural richness of Rhode Island's capital city. Here's a guide to help you make the most of your day:

Visit Roger Williams National Memorial:
Start your day by visiting the Roger Williams National Memorial, which commemorates the life and legacy of the founder of Rhode Island, Roger Williams. Explore the park, learn about religious freedom, and enjoy the serene surroundings.

Tour the Rhode Island State House:
Head to the Rhode Island State House, an architectural gem with a striking marble dome. Take a guided tour to learn about the state's history, see important artifacts, and enjoy panoramic views of Providence from the observation deck.

Stroll along Benefit Street:
Wander through Benefit Street on Providence's East Side, known for its historic architecture and charming colonial-era homes. Benefit Street is home to the Mile of History, showcasing the city's heritage.

Explore College Hill:
Discover College Hill, a historic neighborhood featuring Brown University and the Rhode Island School of Design (RISD). Take a leisurely stroll through the picturesque streets, visit the campuses, and soak in the collegiate atmosphere.

Visit the RISD Museum:
If time allows, visit the RISD Museum to explore its diverse collection of art, including paintings, sculptures, and decorative arts. The museum showcases works from various cultures and time periods.

Lunch on Federal Hill:

Head to Federal Hill, Providence's Little Italy, for lunch. Enjoy authentic Italian cuisine in one of the many restaurants lining the streets. Federal Hill is known for its culinary delights and vibrant atmosphere.

Discover Waterplace Park:
Explore Waterplace Park, a scenic urban park featuring the WaterFire installations along the Woonasquatucket River. Depending on the time of year, you might catch a WaterFire event, an iconic Providence experience.

Take a Gondola Ride:
Enhance your Waterplace Park experience by taking a romantic gondola ride along the river. Enjoy the peaceful ambiance and beautiful views of the city.

Visit the John Brown House Museum:
Immerse yourself in history by touring the John Brown House Museum, a historic mansion reflecting Providence's colonial past. Learn about the city's prominent families and their contributions to American history.

Bike Ride along East Bay Bike Path:
If you enjoy outdoor activities, consider taking a bike ride along the East Bay Bike Path, which stretches from Providence to Bristol. Enjoy scenic views along the Providence River and Narragansett Bay.

Attend a Performance:
Check the schedule for performances at the Providence Performing Arts Center or other local theaters. Catching a show or concert adds entertainment to your day.

Dine on Thayer Street:
Conclude your day trip with dinner on Thayer Street, near Brown University. The area offers a variety of restaurants and cafes, providing a lively atmosphere for the evening.

Remember to check the opening hours and any specific event schedules in advance to make the most of your day trip to Providence Plantations. Enjoy the mix of history, culture, and culinary delights that the city has to offer.

Travel to Providence Rhode Island

Conclusion

Providence, Rhode Island, is a narrative rich in resilience, diversity, and innovation. From its modest beginnings as a haven for religious freedom founded by Roger Williams in the 17th century, Providence has evolved into a vibrant and dynamic city that has played a significant role in shaping American history.

The city's early reliance on maritime trade laid the groundwork for economic prosperity, attracting merchants and entrepreneurs. The Industrial Revolution brought about transformative changes, with Providence becoming a hub for manufacturing and innovation. The city's textile and jewelry industries thrived, leaving an indelible mark on its economic landscape.

Providence's commitment to education and intellectual pursuits is evident through the presence of prestigious institutions like Brown University and the Rhode Island School of Design (RISD). These institutions have contributed not only to the city's intellectual vibrancy but also to its reputation as a center for arts and culture.

Over the years, Providence has embraced its multicultural heritage, with neighborhoods like Federal Hill reflecting the city's diverse immigrant influences. The city's commitment to preserving its historical architecture, seen in districts like Benefit Street, adds a timeless charm to its modern identity.

In recent decades, Providence has undergone revitalization efforts, transforming former industrial spaces into thriving cultural and recreational areas. Waterplace Park and the renaissance of the riverfront with WaterFire events are testaments to the city's commitment to creating vibrant public spaces.

Providence's history is a story of adaptation and reinvention. It has weathered economic shifts, celebrated cultural diversity, and emerged as a city that values its past while embracing progress. As Providence continues to evolve, its history serves as a foundation, guiding the city toward a future that balances innovation, inclusivity, and a celebration of its unique character.

People Who Know Publishing

If you enjoyed, please leave a 5-star Amazon Review

To get a free list of people who knows publishing top places to travel all around the world, click this link
https://bit.ly/peoplewhoknowtravel

Travel to Providence Rhode Island

References

Rcsprinter123, CC BY-SA 3.0 <https://creativecommons.org/licenses/by-sa/3.0>, via Wikimedia Commons
https://pixabay.com/photos/food-sushi-seafood-japan-oriental-3581341/

Made in United States
Troutdale, OR
05/04/2024

19651202R00097